Project Management Institute

D0879254

Stress and Performance in Health Care Project Teams

François Chiocchio, PhD, PMP, CHRP

Paule Lebel, MD, MSc, CRMCC

Pierre-Yves Therriault, PhD, OT(C), CCCPE

Andrée Boucher, MD, FRCPC

Carolyn Hass, MSc, PhD (candidate)

François-Xavier Rabbat, PhD (candidate)

Jean-François Bouchard

Library of Congress Cataloging-in-Publication Data

ISBN: 978-1-935589-64-8

Published by: Project Management Institute, Inc.
                   14 Campus Boulevard
                   Newtown Square, Pennsylvania 19073-3299 USA
                   Phone: +610-356-4600
                   Fax: +610-356-4647
                   Email: customercare@pmi.org
                   Internet: www.PMI.org

©2012 Project Management Institute, Inc. All rights reserved.

PMI", the PMI logo, "PMP", the PMP logo, "PMBOK", "PgMP", "Project Management Journal",
"PM Network", and the PMI Today logo are registered marks of Project Management Institute, Inc.
The Quarter Globe Design is a trademark of the Project Management Institute, Inc. For a compre-
hensive list of PMI marks, contact the PMI Legal Department.

PMI Publications welcomes corrections and comments on its books. Please feel free to send comments on typographical, formatting, or other errors. Simply make a copy of the relevant page of
the book, mark the error, and send it to: Book Editor, PMI Publications, 14 Campus Boulevard,
Newtown Square, PA 19073-3299 USA.

To inquire about discounts for resale or educational purposes, please contact the PMI Book
Service Center.

                   PMI Book Service Center
                   P.O. Box 932683, Atlanta, GA 31193-2683 USA
                   Phone: 1-866-276-4764 (within the U.S. or Canada) or +1-770-280-4129 (globally)
                   Fax: +1-770-280-4113
                   Email: info@bookorders.pmi.org

Printed in the United States of America. No part of this work may be reproduced or transmitted
in any form or by any means, electronic, manual, photocopying, recording, or by any information
storage and retrieval system, without prior written permission of the publisher.

The paper used in this book complies with the Permanent Paper Standard issued by the National
Information Standards Organization (Z39.48—1984).

10 9 8 7 6 5 4 3 2 1

Table of Contents

List of Tables

List of Figures

List of Acronyms and their Translation

All work domains are plagued by the use of acronyms and we are no exception. Because this study was conducted in Quebec – a francophone province of Canada – the use of acronyms is compounded by difficulties in translating names (e.g., in French, institution names are not translatable) and acronyms (e.g., capitalization rules differ in French and English). We chose to keep the original French acronyms in the body of the book. The following list shows these acronyms, their French meaning and an English translation.

List of Acronyms and Their Translations		
Acronym	French	English
CHUM	Centre hospitalier de l'Université de Montréal	Université de Montréal's teaching hospital
CPASS	Centre de pédagogie appliquée aux sciences de la santé de l'Université de Montréal	*Université de Montréal's* Center for Teaching Applied to Health Sciences
CÉRFAS	Comité d'éthique de la recherche de la faculté des arts et des sciences de l'Université de Montréal	*Université de Montréal's* Faculty of Arts & Science's Ethics Review Board
CSSS-SL	Centre de santé et de services sociaux du Sud de Lanaudière	Community health care center of *Lanaudière Sud* region
DPC	Développement professionnel continu	Continuous Professional Development
HMR	Hôpital Maisonneuve-Rosemont	Maisonneuve-Rosemont hospital
IUGM	Institut universitaire de gériatrie de Montréal	*Montréal's* Geriatric Research Institute

Acknowledgments

We are thankful to the Project Management Institute for choosing to finance our project among the 187 submissions it received from research teams across the world following the 2009-2011 cycle's call for proposals. In addition to the financial support, the support of Carla Messikomer (manager, academic resources) and her team and collaborators (Brianne Bangma, Deedra Goldsmith, and Marge Combe) was invaluable. This project was also partially funded by the Social Sciences and Humanities Research Council of Canada (SSHRC).

Thanks also to Donn Greenberg, Barbara Walsh and Dan Goldfischer, of PMI's publishing department for their help in transforming our manuscript into this book.

This project would not have been possible without the participation of the CPASS. Its mission as promoted by a wealth of passionate educators, qualified scientists and practitioners, and devoted administrative personnel was key throughout our project.

Many key players help us gain access to teams:

- Guylaine Tremblay, deputy-director of learning and development directorate (HMR)
- Sylvie Martel, coordinator of professional affaires, multidisciplinary services (HMR)
- Bernard Deschênes, assistant deputy director of organizational transformation and development (CSSS-SL)
- Brigitte St-Pierre, director ethics review committee (CHUM)

Many graduate students worked on this project; we thank them all: Tania Arieira (occupational therapy), Hélène Essiembre (psychology), Isabelle Tremblay (psychology), and Laurence Tremblay (occupational therapy).

Stacey McNulty, PhD, was instrumental with the entire writing process.

We cannot list all those who participated in the research itself in order to maintain their anonymity. We nonetheless thank all of them for believing that our training sessions were going to be beneficial to their respective projects. We know that making time to answer questionnaires and participating in interviews was not easy. Anonymity does not prevent us from naming the institutions who accepted to include teams in our study. Thanks to

- Université de Montréal
- Centre hospitalier de l'Université de Montréal (CHUM)
- Hôpital Maisonneuve-Rosemont (HMR)
- Centre de santé et de services sociaux du Sud de Lanaudière (CSSS-SL)
- Institut universitaire de gériatrie de Montréal (IUGM)

Preface

This book is the result of an interprofessional project team's efforts to improve the health care sector's project success rate. As a team, we share all the characteristics of the teams we wanted to help with our action-research project. Our team members represent multiple professions such as industrial-organizational psychology and organizational behavior, rehabilitation, and medicine – and within medicine, many disciplines, such as endocrinology, geriatrics, and community health care. Like many projects, our team is comprised of people that have different statuses: some are confirmed academics and well-respected practitioners, others are graduate students headed for careers as scientists or practitioners; others play an administrative role. Like almost all teams, our roles evolved throughout the project and some members left the project while other joined. Often we thought we understood each other, only to realize later that in fact we were not quite on the same page. Our project required that we learn from each other, which took time and energy. Like all project teams, we knew going in that we would face important challenges.

There is one main difference between our team and all the teams we worked with during the course of this study: we had knowledge and experience in collaborative work and project-based work. Our team is made up of individuals with a solid track record of success implementing collaborative practices in education or health care – with prizes and recognition to boot. One of us is a Project Management Professional (PMP)® credential holder. We used project management tools and techniques to help us navigate the complexities of our endeavor. Our experience and our knowledge of the research on teamwork, collaboration in health care, and project success in general reminded us of the importance of – and the mechanisms to – span real or socially-constructed boundaries created by professional, disciplinary, status-driven silos. In a nutshell, our project's objective was to help other teams acquire our knowledge and implement simple, yet proven practices so they could improve how they managed their project and ultimately the success of their projects.

What scientists seek reflects their frame of reference, and each discipline teaches its own. To the outsider the divisions and subdivisions of other fields are likely to appear minor and the differences among them trivial. To the dweller within each specialized area, however, the boundaries are important and the differences may be irreconcilable.

Daniel Katz and Robert L. Kahn
The Social Psychology of Organizations,
(1978, p. 186)

Many believe that interdisciplinarity is synonymous with collaboration. It is not.

Julie T. Klein
A Taxonomy of Interdisciplinarity,
(2012, p. 19)

Chapter 1

Why Focus On Interprofessional Health Care Project Teams?

Multiple Paradoxes

A Challenge for Each Paradox

The field of health care is in the midst of a universal transformation. This transformation presents new challenges, but interestingly, as Burns, Bradley, and Weiner put it, "perhaps not so new challenges and opportunities" (2012, p. xi). On the one hand, health care is more than ever focused on providing the most effective care in the most efficient way. On the other hand, health care's growing complexity requires that an ever-increasing number of highly specialized individuals work together to solve increasingly complex problems. These two trends collide and require all those working in health care—physicians and nurses, many other health care professional and technicians, managers, support staff, IT technicians, etc.—to continuously, reflexively, and relentlessly work to maximize the way they collaborate with each other. However, several paradoxes hamper health care workers' efforts to collaborate.

Ask your colleagues and co-workers what collaboration is. Ask them to give you examples of what they or others did in good—or not so good—situations where people worked collaboratively. Everybody will have a definition and a few good stories—no matter what their job is or their position in the organization. Collaboration is like parenting. Parenting is the most difficult job in the world. We know what it is, we know it is complex, we know we need to do it better; yet we seem to never quite grasp all its complexities, and feel we are failing more often than not. Similarly, collaboration is not new and we already know what to do to be better at it: people must learn to work together. Yet, we rarely fully succeed. There's the first paradox.

As the whole of health care (re)focuses its attention on increased and improved collaboration, organizations and their employees are challenged to improve their day-to-day work. Hence, as managers, health care professionals and all others who contribute to deliver health services struggle to work collaboratively in the first place, they must also understand enough about collaboration to address needed improvements, solve complex service coordination and delivery issues, and do so across management, professional, and disciplinary boundaries. In other words, to improve collaborative practices, health care workers must also work well collaboratively. But how can we succeed at improving collaborative practices if, as in the first paradox, we have difficulties with collaboration in the first place? This is the second paradox.

Health care professionals are trained to deliver services. Service work is complex and involves multiple, relatively short, discreet work episodes (Sundstrom, McIntyre, Halfhill, & Richards, 2000) aimed directly at patients (e.g., medical staff caring for critically ill patients) or at other people in the organization (e.g., radiologists providing X-ray reports to physicians) (Chiocchio, Dubé, & Lebel, 2012). From the organizations' perspective, service work is ongoing because units have predictable operations and well-defined processes and procedures. Collaboration's main challenge in service work is the acute need for coordination between specialties (Grieshaber, 1997) so that knowledge and expertise converge in high quality decision-making designed to adequately respond to patients' needs (Sicotte, D'Amour, & Moreault, 2002).

While working collaboratively is difficult (first paradox) and working collaboratively to continuously improve collaborative practices is also difficult (second paradox), health care workers have some measure of success improving health care service delivery because the challenges of continuous improvement do not depart substantially from their training, knowledge, and experiences, and thus from the regular ways they are trained to solve day-to-day problems. In a sense, continuous improvement is the status quo. Ambiguity remains, however. Since health care workers were—and still are—always engaged in continuous improvement, how is it then that the problem is not solved and that it is still necessary to improve? This is the third paradox.

One reason for the unremitted need to improve on collaborative practices—in addition to increasing complexity of health care needs—is that in some instances, gradual improvements are not enough. Sometimes, abrupt, radical, and disruptive changes are required. While continuous improvements involve much of the same processes health professionals are trained to carry out, the challenge is much steeper when radical change is necessary because radical change improvement requires distancing oneself from the status quo. Henriksen and Dayton remind us of the difficulties of challenging the status quo: "Whether it is adopting a new clinical process, designing a new product, or managing one's portfolio of mutual funds, it is very difficult to break away from the seemingly magnetic pull of the status quo. Maintaining the status quo is comfortable and requires no further action. Breaking away and taking a different course of action requires decision making, uncertainty, doubt, and renewed responsibility." (2006, p. 1544). In our view, these difficulties are compounded by the fact that implementing a radical change operates on a completely different logic than "regular" service work and continuous improvement: the logic of a project.

A project has five essential features (Chiocchio, Dubé, et al., 2012; Turner & Müller, 2003). First, contrary to continuous improvements which are by definition ongoing, a project is undertaken to deliver some kind of beneficial change at a given time. It follows that at some point in time in the future, the change will be delivered. Hence, a project is a temporary endeavor. Second, a project is a transient organization within the organization. A project is carried out by a team (unlike crews or people involved in shift work) characterized as a stable core of individuals assembled across functions, disciplines, or professions that self-organize over months or years in parallel to their regular duties. Third, the change to be delivered represents a high degree of novelty—nothing quite like it was ever done by these people for that purpose at that time. Fourth, because of the novelty and uniqueness of the proposed change, both the deliverables and the processes to deliver them are elaborated progressively as the project unfolds in time. The fifth feature is very salient when it comes to describing projects in health care. Although ultimately a project's outcome is aimed at patients, a project's outcome is actually delivered to the organization first (which signals the end of the project). In other words, it is only once the project's outcome is implemented and becomes "the new way we work now" that it starts exerting its impact on patients.

One major problem in health care is that most of its workers are largely unaware of differences between service work and project work, and do not have a clear understanding of what these differences entail. Health care workers are trained to enact their expertise so that they can help many patients in real time on an ongoing basis. In other words, the beneficiaries of health care workers' expertise are patients. When interprofessional collaboration is deficient, it is an organization, a part of an organization, a system of services, or a unit of health care workers that need fixing and healing, not patients. Sadly, people in health care are inefficient at focusing on understanding and addressing process issues and inadequate system interdependencies (Henriksen & Dayton, 2006).

As with the previous paradoxes, ambiguities and contradictions arise here too. While all recognize that projects to improve interprofessional collaboration require the knowledge and expertise of the very professionals embedded in the system that needs fixing, their expertise remains an unrefined raw material for project work until two changes occur. First, their expertise and knowledge must be translated from experiences in ongoing service work to building solutions in the course of temporary progressively elaborated project work. Second, the target of the expertise must shift from healing patients to healing an organization (or a part of an organization). So, while projects cannot do without professionals to deliver a change in interprofessional collaboration, how can health care workers appropriately engage in project work if they are unaware of what project work is or entails? Furthermore, even if all health care workers were fully aware of all the intricacies of project work, *nobody* knows how to transcend "regular "professional expertise in to the kind of expertise health care professional must inject to a project for it to succeed. There is the fourth paradox.

Our analysis of the difficulties with managing interprofessional project teams in health care can be summarized into these four paradoxes. First, although apparently clear, collaboration is actually very complex. Second, professionals need good interprofessional collaboration to improve collaborative practices. Third, since continuous improvement in interprofessional collaboration is at the core of what being a professional is, why aren't things "improved" already? Finally, how can professionals inject their expertise in a project without the knowledge or ability to reframe their expertise in a way pertinent for the needs of the project? More fundamentally, how can they do so if they are unaware of what a project is?

Embedded Paradoxes

In addition to the challenges specific to each of these paradoxes, there is a fifth paradox: a successful project is dependent upon resolving all four paradoxes. To successfully deliver change projects in the way health care workers collaborate interprofessionally, they must solve the fourth paradox of figuring out how to transcend their expertise in order to help the project, despite the fact they might not even know they need to morph—or have morphed—into a project team. To do that, health care workers must "step up" their continuous improvements efforts, despite the fact these efforts were not successful, at least up to the point the need for a radical change arose. To "step up" efforts necessary to deliver the change, health care workers must collaborate exceptionally well interprofessionally. Although health care workers have an intuitive knowledge and accumulated wisdom of what interprofessional collaboration is and how to improve it, interprofessional collaboration remains somewhat an elusive reality.

These paradoxes make life difficult for members of interprofessional health care project team, hindering their health, and their ability to manage projects successfully.

Why This Book?

This book is about helping health care workers spin out of these intertwined paradoxes and succeed at their projects. What you are reading stems from our passion for and experience with interprofessional health care project teams. In our experience, health care workers involved in radical change endeavors, although correct in their analysis of the need for change, are ill equipped to plow through the challenges of a project. Our observation of health care workers' efforts to radically improve how the work is performed in their area or unit is that they deploy two types of solutions depending on the extent to which they understand the difference between service and project work.

When those differences are unknown or unrecognized, health care workers take footing on their usual concepts of work (i.e., service work and continuous improvements) and apply them to implementing radical changes. Grieshaber states it differently: "policies, procedures, and rules are not appropriate" to manage a project (1997, p. 25). In other words, they "more intensely" engage in continuous improvements efforts, yet fall prey to our third paradox without actually being able to clearly or satisfactorily implement a change. To use a metaphor, health care workers used to walking on trails simply "walk harder" when they realize they are going uphill. The steeper the hill, the more vigorous the walk. Before long—and especially if the hill is actually a mountain—"walking harder" ends up being less about walking and more about sitting on the side of the trail catching their breath.

When health care workers have intuitive knowledge that the change initiative is a different kind of work than what they are used to, they make efforts to remove themselves from day-to-day hustle and bustle in order to "meet." They recognize they need to "plan" and they assign "tasks" to others on "the team," all the while not fully grasping the meaning of these concepts and activities in terms of project management. In other words, these steps are part of project management, but they are usually not done sufficiently well for projects to succeed.

Then they start. Before long—especially if people realize the "plan" is actually not working, and therefore "wrong"—people get frustrated and often fall back to continuous improvement mode. To continue with our metaphor, when people realize the trek will not be on flat trails but uphill, they go buy fancy shoes, maybe a walking stick. Then they start climbing. However, buying special shoes is not mountain climbing, and even the best shoes inflict blisters. Similarly, intuitive and expedited planning is not sufficient to manage a project.

All this wasted energy takes a toll on health care workers. One of our recent studies suggest that compared to those not involved in projects, health care workers involved in projects are more prone to higher levels of psychological distress and lower lever of psychological well-being (Chiocchio et al., 2010). Because the study also compared health care workers to workers in a field used to managing projects, and thus with people trained in project management, we thought that training in project management would help health care project teams succeed in their projects and reduce the toll project work exerts on their psychological health. We also believed that working on a project would be an excellent way to emphasize interprofessional collaboration. Consequently, we devised training that combines knowledge transfer and skill building in interprofessional collaboration *and* in project management.

Our interest and passion for these topics goes beyond training and development and there is another reason why we wrote this book. Apparent from our vision of the challenges health care workers face when working interprofessionally in project teams, problems are many and far reaching. As academics, we are also keen in contributing new knowledge on the health of health care workers, on how they work collaboratively, and on how their projects succeed or fail. This book is a response to the fact that not much research has been conducted on interprofessional health care project teams.

Target Audience and Objectives of this Book

In the true tradition of action-research—where uncompromisingly solid research is used to transfer knowledge to potential users of its results—we aim at providing human resource managers, project management office representatives, and members of interprofessional health care project teams with usable evidence to improve project management. In doing so we have purposefully chose to report *a wide array of results in the most simple manner possible*. As such, this book is not a long scientific article (or a series of scientific articles) academics might be accustomed to where, generally speaking, a few topics or variables are examined with complex methods. To the contrary, we rely on verbatim testimony and on one simple yet powerful statistical index to convey as much information possible: the correlation. Those unfamiliar with correlations can find an explanation of this statistical marvel in Appendix 1. Academics will recognize in what we present descriptive and univariate evidence (drawbacks to a univariate approach is briefly discussed in Appendix 9). We view this evidence as a starting point to multivariate hypotheses regarding how project workload, job demands, job control, and social support interact in the understudied context of interprofessional health care project teams.

Furthermore, research is often portrayed as hermetic and largely irrelevant. Our study is a testimony of the pertinence and utility of applied research conducted in partnership with the *milieu*. Our study comes in sharp contrast to the vast majority of studies that aim at addressing dynamic problems but only use static methods (i.e., cross-sectional data collection and analysis). We went to great lengths to capture the complexity of the aforementioned phenomena with measurements at multiple times across the life cycle of projects. Finally, most studies use a single conceptualization and a single method to trace phenomena. Specifically, a majority of studies use a positivist perspective and quantitative questionnaires to describe, understand, and predict phenomena. We invested much energy to examine our topics through a parallel process based on a constructivist qualitative stance. Triangulating research results that stem from two distinct theories is exciting from a scientific standpoint and—we believe—better.

With the target audience and general means by which we will govern our analysis in mind, it is important to state our objectives.

- Our first specific objective is to describe and report on our attempts to create and measure the impact of a training program designed to transfer project management and interprofessional collaboration knowledge. *For us, managing a project and collaborating interprofessionally are inextricably related; both are necessary to the other.*
- Our second objective is to describe and examine how the additional demands brought on by project workload, job demands, decision latitude (i.e., the power one has to make decisions and act accordingly), skill discretion (i.e., the autonomy one has in how one carries out his or her tasks) and perceived stress impacts important phenomena pertinent to teamwork of interprofessional health care project teams. *We hope to shed some light on what fosters or impedes successful project completion in the health care context.*

Organization of the Book

The organization of the book is straightforward. Chapter 2, titled "Interprofessional teams in health care: A response to complexity," will dive into the issue of interprofessional collaboration. This is necessary because of our belief that health care sector challenges stem from embedded paradoxes regarding interprofessional collaboration, and that interprofessional collaboration is the great unknown, the process, and the end state all at once.

Chapters 3 provides an overview of our study process and general structure of the data we collected. It is important to understand our overarching study process since we decided to organize and present results in three distinct chapters.

Specifically, Chapter 4 tackles the issue of training health care workers in interprofessinal collaboration project management and if what we did actually works. Chapter 5 examines more broadly the issue of what effect the relationships workload, stress, and coping have on other important phenomena such as collaboration, social support, and performance. Chapter 6 examines the retrospective accounts of the people we trained and surveyed to better understand their behaviors and team dynamics.

In Chapter 7, titled "Addressing paradoxes of interprofessional health care project teams," we step back, summarize our findings, return to our paradoxes and assess whether we succeeded in our own project.

Chapter 2

Interprofessional Teams in Health Care: A Response to Complexity

From Complex Health Problems to an Efficiency-Seeking Health Network

Challenges

Various challenges have fostered the rise of interprofessional collaboration in health care. The first is complexity. The growing prevalence of chronic diseases and an aging population, precarious psychosocial conditions of vulnerable clients, and increasing consumption of drugs with potential adverse effects, are only some of the reasons warranting the pooling of professional health expertise to meet the population's complex health needs. The need to implement integrated service networks to counter the fragmentation of care and lack of intervention coordination between primary care and specialized services calls for inter-institutional and inter-sectorial collaborations (e.g., health sector with law, environment, labor, and housing sectors) (Fleury, Grenier, Cazal, & Perrault, 2008; Fleury, Tremblay, Nguyen, & Bordeleau, 2007). As stressed by Mitchell, Parker, Giles, and White, "there is increasing pressure calling for collaborative interprofessional work" (2010, p. 4). Such phenomenon stem from the recognition that, in difficult cases, and in the context of complex health organizations, no single individual has the capacity to deliver high-quality care (Segal, 1994). Unsurprisingly, collaborative practices are now embedded in policy (Cunningham & Dunn, 2001).

The second challenge is patient safety. In the patient safety literature, it is widely recognized that team performance is paramount in providing safe patient care. Poor coordination among providers at various levels of the organization appears to affect the quality and safety of patient care (e.g., delays in testing or treatment, conflicting information). Thus, teamwork has become a focus of system-based interventions to improve patient safety (Manser, 2009).

The third challenge is organizational sustainability. The challenges of developing learning and attractive organizations to promote recruitment and retention of health care workers call for the use of teams, the optimal functioning of which is a pledge for job satisfaction, professional development, and personal growth.

To address these challenges, interprofessional collaborative practices have emerged as an imperative. Teams working in mental health (Kingdon, 1992), rehabilitation (Strasser et al., 2005), and geriatrics (Rich et al., 1995; Young et al., 2011) were pioneers in the area. More recently, significant efforts have been achieved among teams specializing in chronic diseases such as cerebrovascular accident/stroke (Canadian Stroke Network, 2010) and cancer (Programme de lutte contre le cancer, 1997), to improve their efficiency through the production of clinical guidelines, including interprofessional collaboration dimensions. Primary care teams have taken the same path (Goldman, Meuser, Lawrie, Rogers, & Reeves, 2010; Goldman, Meuser, Rogers, & Reeves, 2010).

An Answer to Challenges: Interprofessional Collaboration as an Emerging Concept

Difficulties with conceptualizations of collaboration

Defining collaboration is not an easy thing to do. A recent review points to seven problems practitioners and academics face when focusing on collaboration (Chiocchio, Grenier, O'Neill, Savaria, & Willms, 2012). Of those seven problems, five are directly relevant here. First, it is not rare that authors do not define collaboration or its relevant constructs even when they advocate them. Second, not everybody has the same lens; some regard collaboration as a macro phenomenon while others understand it at a more micro level. Third, it is not rare to find similar definitions under different labels or similar labels with different meanings. Fourth, some define collaboration with other constructs, without defining these other constructs, which is even more complicated, given the third problem. The fifth problem is that some offer internally consistent definitions within a particular study, yet that do not generalize well across studies.

The importance of teams, teamwork and taskwork

In our view, interprofessional collaboration is subsumed within the general idea of what a team is and what it is to work in a team. Modern definitions of teams go beyond the basic premise of common goals and interdependencies. Summarizing many writings on teams across fields and work settings, Kozlowski and Ilgen state that "A team can be defined as (a) two or more individuals who (b) socially interact (face-to-face or, increasingly, virtually); (c) possess one or more common goals; (d) are brought together to perform organizationally relevant tasks; (e) exhibit interdependencies with respect to workflow, goals, and outcomes; (f) have different roles and responsibilities; and (g) are together embedded in an encompassing organizational system, with boundaries and linkages to the broader system context and task environment" (2006, p. 79). More recently, yet still examining definitions of teams across fields and work settings, an incrementally more intricate definition of teams appeared which adds to Kozlowski and Ilgen's many elements—that teams are complex entities whose members influence each other through the competencies they enact, and must interact socially, dynamically, recursively, and adaptively (Salas, Priest, Stagl, Sims, & Burke, 2007).

These overarching definitions are echoed in definitions found in the health care literature. For instance, the World Health Organization defines a health care work group as "A group of persons who share a common health goal and common objectives determined by community needs, to which the achievement of each member of the work group contributes, in a coordinated manner, in accordance with his/her competence and skills and respecting the functions of others." (World Health Organization, 1985).

Even more specifically, Drinka & Clark (2000) define an interdisciplinary health care team (IHCT) as a group of individuals with diverse training and backgrounds who work together as an identified unit or system. Team members consistently collaborate to solve patient problems that are too complex to be solved by one discipline or many disciplines in sequence. In order to provide care as efficiently as possible, an IHCT creates formal and informal structures that encourage collaborative problem solving. Team members determine the team's mission and common goals, work interdependently to define and treat patient problems, and learn to accept and capitalize on disciplinary differences, differential power, and overlapping roles. To accomplish these, they share leadership that is appropriate to the presenting problem and promote the use of differences for confrontation and collaboration. They also use differences of opinion and problems to evaluate the team's work and its development.

Defining interprofessional collaboration and related constructs

Team members enact taskwork and teamwork (Marks, Mathieu, & Zaccaro, 2001). Taskwork refers to the things people do that relate to the competencies they acquired through their training (e.g., a radiologist uses special equipment to extract interpretable images, a nurse injects medication intravenously to an intensive care unit patient). Teamwork is how team members work to combine their thoughts, actions, and feelings to coordinate and adapt, and to reach a common goal.

Hence, teams—as complex as they are—exist to have their members perform their taskwork more efficaciously through teamwork. As such, what is meant by collaboration in general, and interprofessional collaboration in particular, is in fact what is implicitly understood as "good" teamwork. For example, interprofessional collaboration is often qualified as a set of "positive" relationships and interactions that allow professionals to share their knowledge, expertise, and experience for the better good of those in need of care (D'Amour, Sicotte, & Lévy, 1999).

Many authors have suggested definitions of interprofessional collaboration for health care teams (Table 2.1). Several commonalities emerge from such definitions: i) a common target (mission and objectives) to answer patients and families' needs; ii) the pooling of various expertise; iii) shared problem solving and decision making; iv) coherent and coordinated actions; v) smooth and efficient communication mechanisms; vi) partnership with patients and families, considered as full members of the team; vii) team self-assessment and continuous improvement processes.

Pointing to communalities across domains and work settings when it comes to understanding collaboration, it is worth noting that Hoegl, Weinkauf, and Gemuenden (2004) studied a six-factor model of collaboration in research and development project teams: communication, coordination, balance of member contributions, mutual support, effort and cohesion.

Another model aligned on collaboration being a teamwork process and validated in many work context defines collaboration as the interplay of situation-appropriate uses of four interrelated sub-processes: teamwork communication, synchronicity, explicit coordination, and implicit coordination (Chiocchio, Grenier, et al., 2012). In addition to viewing teamwork

Table 2.1: Definitions of Interprofessional Collaboration and Related Concepts

Collaborative Practice (Way, Jones, & Busing, 2000)	• An interprofessional process for communication and decision making that enables the separate and shared knowledge and skills of care providers to synergistically influence client/patient care.
Collaborative Patient-Centered Practice (Herbert, 2005)	• A practice orientation, a way for health care professionals working together and with their patients. It involves the continuous interaction of two or more professionals or disciplines, organized into a common effort, to solve or explore common issues with the best possible participation of the patient. Collaborative patient-centered practice is designed to promote the active participation of each discipline in patient care. It enhances patient- and family-centered goals and values, provides mechanisms for continuous communication among care givers, optimizes staff participation in clinical decision making within and across disciplines, and fosters respect for disciplinary contributions of all professionals.
Interprofessional Collaboration in Social Work (Bronstein, 2003)	• Interprofessional collaboration is comprised of five constructs, namely interdependence, newly created professional activities, flexibility, collective ownership of goals, and reflection on process. These constructs relate to contextual variables such as professional role, structural characteristics, personal characteristics, and a history of collaboration.
Multi-Disciplinary Teams (Lowe and O'Hara 2000)	• Authors outline structures and processes that may help established multidisciplinary teams: coordination and communication, planned regular meetings, frequency of meetings, collaborative decision making, and shared goal-planning.
Interprofessional collaboration (Canadian Interprofessional Health Collaborative, 2010; Orchard, 2008)	• A partnership between a team of health providers and a client in a participatory collaborative and coordinated approach to shared decision-making pertaining to health and social issues. The interprofessional team integrates and values, as a partner, the input of a patient or family in the design and implementation of care and services. The patient remains in control of his or her care and is provided access to the knowledge and skills of team members to arrive at a realistic team-shared plan for care and access to the resources required to achieve the plan. The patient is seen as an expert of his or her own personal experience and is critical in shaping realistic care plans.

communication as an exchange of information between a sender and a receiver (McIntyre & Salas, 1995), this model further defines teamwork communication as a process focused on establishing interactions and enhancing their quality (Kozlowski & Bell, 2003) so that members share ideas freely, listen, understand, and receive and give feedback. Because teamwork cannot be described without addressing how work and interactions between team members unfold over time (Bedwell et al., 2012) the second sub-process is synchronicity—that is a process by which team members perform their tasks on time (i.e., timeliness) and in accordance with others' tasks (i.e., timing). Based on Salas and Fiore's (2004) work on team cognition, this model further defines two sub-processes. Explicit coordination is a process by which team members exchange information on roles and tasks (i.e., who does what). Implicit coordination is a process by which team members anticipate others' needs and adapt to situations and people without resorting to explicit coordination.

From multidisciplinarity, to interdisciplinarity, to transdisciplinarity

In order to optimize efficiency of health teams working with clients displaying complex health and psychosocial needs, interprofessional health care teams must progressively transform their practice from a multidisciplinary mode to an interdisciplinary, perhaps transdisciplinary mode (Table 2.2). Multidisciplinarity implies team members add their knowledge and expertise to the problem at hand. Interdisciplinarity implies team members integrate knowledge and expertise using cross-boundary translation. Transdisciplinarity goes further and advocates team members fully integrate each others' knowledge and expertise because of vanishing boundaries.

Table 2.2: Types of Teams and Degree of Collaboration Within a Team Based on a Continuum of Professional Autonomy

Multi-Disciplinary Teams	• Several different professionals work on the same project but independently or in parallel (juxtaposition of various professionals and competencies), implying some coordination of actions.
Inter-Disciplinary Teams	• Implies a greater degree of collaboration among members, where themes and schemes become shared and integrated – not solely juxtaposition, but rather a common space, cohesion, and shared ownership. Refers to a more structured entity, with common goals and decision-making processes – integration of knowledge and expertise, solving of more complex problems, more flexibility, more open professional boundaries (interdependent relationships).
Trans-Disciplinary Teams	• Consensus-seeking and opening up of professional boundaries is key – boundaries are blurred or vanished. Involves deliberate exchange of knowledge, skills, and expertise that transcends traditional disciplinary boundaries.

Note: This table derives from the work of D'Amour, Ferrada-Videla, San Martin Rodriguez, & Beaulieu (2005).

This transition implies increasing interdependence between team members for the benefit of shared expertise and greater efficiency and health care quality. Results must be quickly tangible so that professionals, especially physicians, accept the inevitable loss of some of their professional autonomy associated with such functioning mode.

Interprofessional collaboration: A constellation of practices

Interprofessional collaboration practice takes highly diversified forms in clinical contexts. Some examples include:

- Joint assessment of patient health by two care providers from different professions, and development and implementation of interdisciplinary intervention plans;
- Interprofessional clinical rounds in hospital medical-surgical units, such as intensive care and coronary care units;
- Reviewing of adverse events, including medication errors, nosocomial infections, wounds, and patient falls;
- Interprofesional therapeutic education to patients;
- Interprofessional consultation in person or through videoconferencing;
- Application of interprofessional clinical protocols, interprofessional training (journal clubs, case conferences, simulations, etc.);
- Continuous improvement learning and activities.

In order to be effective, these various situations where interprofessional collaboration is paramount must be based on partnerships with patients and families, process formalization, shared administrative and clinical leadership, clearly defined roles and responsibilities, communication adapted to situational constraints of various care providers, and prompt and efficient conflict management focused on finding win-win solutions.

One of the most important model of collaboration is that of D'Amour, Goulet, Ladadie, San Martin-Rodriguez, & Pineault (2008). They developed a four-dimensional model of collaboration characterized by ten indicators specific to primary care (Table 2.3). These collaboration indicators were shown to be valid in various studies. The model enables researchers to analyze collaboration in relationship with clinical outcomes. The model is

Table 2.3: The Four-Dimensional Model of Collaboration

Dimensions	Definitions	Indicators
Governance	Leadership functions that support collaboration. Gives direction and support to professionals as they implement innovations related to interprofessional and interorganizational collaborative practices.	Centrality Leadership Support for innovation Connectivity
Formalization	Extent to which documented procedures communicating desired outputs and behaviors exist and are used.	Formalization tools Information exchange
Shared Goals and Vision	Existence of common goals and their appropriation by the team, the recognition of divergent motives and multiple allegiances, and of the diversity in definitions and expectations regarding collaboration.	Goals Client-centered orientation vs. other allegiances
Internalization	Awareness by professionals of their interdependencies and of the importance of managing them; translates into a sense of belonging, knowledge of each other's values and disciplines, and mutual trust.	Mutual acquaintance Trust

Note: This table derives from the work of D'Amour et al (2008).

also useful for professionals and administrators because they can diagnose collaboration problems and implement commensurate interventions.

Positive Outcomes of Interprofessional Collaboration

There is ample evidence of the effectiveness of interprofessional collaboration in terms of patient, organizational, and staff outcomes.

Manser's (2009) review of literature on teamwork and patient safety reveals that

- Teamwork plays an important role in the causation and prevention of adverse events;
- Staff's perceptions of teamwork and attitude toward safety-relevant team behaviors are related to the quality and safety of patient care;
- Perceptions of teamwork and leadership style are associated with staff well-being, which may impact clinicians' ability to provide safe patient care;
- Specific patterns of communication, coordination, and leadership are related to high clinical performance.

O'Leary et al. (2011) showed in a controlled trial that structured interdisciplinary rounds in a tertiary care academic hospital reduced the rate of adverse events, mainly adverse drug events (0.9 per 100 patient-days versus 2.8 and 2.1 for the control units). These are promising results, given inherent characteristics of these medical-surgical units. For example, there are several important and unique barriers to effective communication among health care professionals in these units: teams are large and formed in an ad hoc fashion, and team membership is dynamic and dispersed. Physicians, nurses, pharmacists, and other team members typically care for multiple patients simultaneously and work in shifts of rotations, resulting in team membership variability and instability.

In addition to enhancing a patient-focused approach, interprofessional collaboration is also key in facilitating recovery, reducing complications and mortality (Canadian Health Services Research Foundation, 2006; Mitchell et al., 2010). In addition, these authors show that interprofessional collaboration helps reduce medications per patient and improves medication appropriateness and compliance.

Interprofessional collaboration also improves various organizational outcomes such as avoidance of duplication and fragmentation, fewer out-of-hours consultations and hospital visits, reduced hospital length of stay, reduced admission to emergency or intensive-care units, reduction in health costs, and enhanced innovation potential (Canadian Health Services Research Foundation, 2006; Mitchell et al., 2010). These publications also emphasize that health care workers engaged in interprofessional collaboration experience richer roles and improved job satisfaction, and are less prone to quitting (i.e., reduced turnover).

Pitfalls Associated with the Implementation of Collaborative Practices

Although the outcomes are undeniable, there are several obstacles to implementing interprofessional collaborative practices, and these are inherent to organizations, teams as well as care providers. Several authors (Goldman, Meuser, Rogers, et al., 2010; Headrick, Wilcock, & Batalden, 1998; Walsh et al., 2010) report a litany of issues and pitfalls encountered by managers and clinical care providers in achieving interprofessional collaboration, including:

- Lack of time, space and resources;
- Differences in history and culture of organizations;
- Historical interprofessional and intraprofessional rivalries;
- Differences in language and jargon;
- Differences in schedules and professional routines;
- Varying levels of preparation, qualifications, and status;
- Differences in requirements, regulations, and norms of professional education;
- Fear of diluted professional identity;
- Differences in accountability;
- Payment and rewards;
- Concerns regarding clinical responsibility;
- Lack of role clarity as well as of organizational or professional leadership;
- Inadequate communication between professionals.

Recent observations regarding the influence of team compositional diversity on team performance stress that such diversity, which is desired for solving complex problems, can, if not structured, lead to negative results (Mitchell et al., 2010). Developing effective collaborative practices, therefore, requires sustained efforts at all levels, based on shared organizational and professional missions and values.

Turning Towards Project Work

The preceding discussion can be captured in the following way. First, interprofessional collaboration is necessary, yet it remains a complex and evolving construct difficult to enact successfully or consistently. Second, interprofessional collaboration is occurring in all forms of health care services because people recognize it is the best form of teamwork, but also because it will produce truly positive impacts on patients, organizations, and worker moral. Parallel to perceived and actual benefits, there are a number of pitfalls that hinder interprofessional collaboration and/or its implementation. Third, models exist that pinpoint determinants of successful interprofessional collaboration, namely: governance, formalization, shared goals and vision, and internalization. Finally, there is evidence for the pertinence of these factors in the context of continuous health care service delivery.

As stated in the introduction, our contention in this book is that interprofessional collaboration also takes place in situations when health care teams engage in project work. And although ongoing health care service delivery, and more generally clinical settings, have been well served by studies on interprofessional collaboration, the same cannot be true for project work. With the possible exception of research and development projects involving researchers and clinicians, there is scarce evidence—none, to our knowledge— that contributes to improve our understanding of change initiative projects undertaken by diversified teams of professionals and other key health care providers. As we will see in Chapters 4, 5, and 6, we will seek to fill this gap with measures and analysis commensurate with governance (e.g., organizational support and social support), formalization (e.g., project charters, planning and risk analysis), shared goals and vision (e.g., goal clarity), and internalization (e.g., task interdependence and collaborative processes).

Chapter 3

Study Process, Projects and Participants

Ethics Reviews

The research protocol developed by the research team was presented to a first ethics review board (i.e., CÉRFAS), which awarded a certificate of ethics for the study. This certificate did not, however, cover all aspects required by health institutions. Hence, we had to apply to other review boards in each institution, namely:

- Centre hospitalier de l'Université de Montréal (CHUM)
- Hôpital Maisonneuve-Rosemont (HMR)
- Centre de santé et de services sociaux du Sud de Lanaudière (CSSS-SL)
- Institut universitaire de gériatrie de Montréal (IUGM)

Although each institution and hospital had its own certification requirements, we were able to fast-track the ethics review processes in each facility as our research showed no major risk: it did not involve patients or information from patients' files and did not involve experimental trials (drug samples or other medical interventions). A training project or improvement of practice for clinicians, not patients, as was often the case for the teams participating in our research, is generally considered low risk. Certificates of ethics of each of these institutions have been awarded quickly.

In addition, more and more health professions require their practitioners to undertake continuing education to ensure their knowledge and skills stay current. To this end, it is usually the directors of teaching hospitals who oversee, coordinate, and manage training projects or communicate with partners for such projects. For the CHUM and HMR, for example, we were approved by their respective continuous education directorates, since the projects proposed by the interested teams involved training and were therefore considered for continuous professional development.

Recruitment and Admissibility

As our research project was conducted jointly with the CPASS, working in collaboration with various hospitals, we were able to access top management of several hospitals. Subsequently, human resources, continuous education, and interprofessional care directorates disseminated information to clinical teams to inform them of the existence of the research. In most cases, the research team then met with small groups of key people in organizations to explain the study, its requirements in terms of research and project eligibility, in addition to the sequence of training.

Criteria used in some of our past research (e.g., Chiocchio, Grenier, et al., 2012) determined whether people identified by health care facilities' management could be included in the study. Specifically, a team is a collection of individuals who are interdependent in their tasks, who share responsibility for outcomes, who see themselves and who are seen by others as an intact social entity embedded in one or more larger social systems, and who manage their relationships across organizational boundaries (S. G. Cohen & Bailey, 1997). Furthermore, they had to be an interprofessional team working on a project. A team is interprofessional if it is comprised of three or more members of different professions or disciplines such as physicians, nurses, pharmacists, various health professionals, managers, stakeholders, and community workers (Heinemann, 2002). Finally, a project is a temporary process designed to create something unique and whereby the process, its objective/ purpose, or both, are progressively elaborated. Temporariness implies that there is a known start date and an anticipated end date, as well as that a project ends when its objectives are met or when it is intentionally terminated. Uniqueness refers to the outcome of the project, either as a new product or new service. Progressive elaboration is the combination of temporariness and uniqueness (Project Management Institute, 2008). Moreover, in order to be eligible, each team was required to have an approximated duration of one year in order to respect the temporal demands of the research project.

Eleven interprofessional health care project teams (each with approximately seven members, including one who has a coordination/project management role) were recruited from major university (i.e., teaching) and health care facilities in and around Montréal, Québec, Canada. Once included in the study, team members received an electronic consent form and proceeded to answering the first questionnaire prior to the first training session.

Study Design and Process

As successfully applied in previous project management research (e.g., Chiocchio, 2007; Chiocchio & Lafrenière, 2009), this study uses both quantitative and qualitative methods. This mixed methodology serves to alleviate some of the many challenges associated with measuring occupational stress (for a review of these challenges, see Ganster, 2008). On the one hand, a quantitative longitudinal quasi-experimental design was applied. Validated questionnaires, some in paper-and-pencil format (i.e., the training efficacy component of our study) and some administered online using a password-protected protocol (i.e., the job demands, job control, and stress component of our study), were used. On the other hand, individual interviews were conducted at the end of the process (i.e., the job demands, job control and stress component of our study).

Figure 1 shows a schematic view of the research design and Table 3.1 shows an overview of measurements for each component of the study.

The mean duration from the time participants answered questionnaire A to the time they participated in the final interview was 38.87 weeks ($SD = 14.26$).

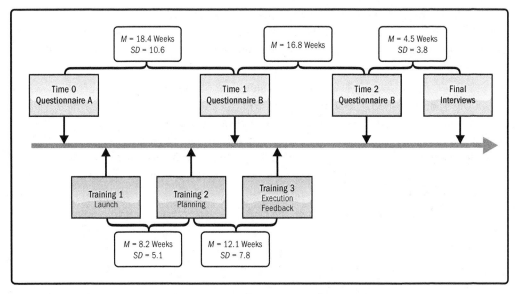

Figure 1: - Schematic View of the Research Design and Process

Table 3.1: Synthesis of Measurements.

Study Component	Construct Measured, Instrument Name, and Author
	Training Efficacy
Pre-Post Self-Efficacy	• Self-Efficacy Regarding Human Factors* • Self-Efficacy Regarding Project Management Factors*
Reactions to Training	• Satisfaction (Beaulieu, in progress) • Transferability (Beaulieu, in progress)
	Demand, Control and Perceived Stress: A Longitudinal Quantitative Examination
Time 0 – Questionnaire A	• Supporting Infrastructure (Spreitzer, 1996) • Project Management Maturity (Kerzner, 1998) • Conflict Handling (De Dreu, Evers, Beersma, Kluwer, & Nauta, 2001) • Informational Role Self-Efficacy (Chiocchio, Dubé, et al., 2012)
Times 1 and 2 – Questionnaire B	• Job Demands and Job Control (Bosma et al., 1997) • Perceived Stress (S. Cohen, Kamarck, & Mermelstein, 1983) • Psychological Health: Anxiety and depression (Warr, 2005) • Goal Similarity (Jehn, 1995) • Task Interdependency (Campion, Medsker, & Higgs, 1993) • Goal Clarity (Sawyer, 1992) • Intragroup Trust (Simons & Peterson, 2000) • Project Commitment (Hoegl et al., 2004) • Social Support Provision (Cutrona & Russell, 1987) • Collaboration (Chiocchio, Grenier, et al., 2012) • Interdisciplinary Collaboration (Vinokur-Kaplan, 1995) • Conflicts (Jehn & Mannix, 2001) • Individual and Team Behavioral Performance (Griffin, Neal, & Parker, 2007) • Regular Assessment of Project Progression (Stratman & Roth, 2002) • Project Performance (Gelbard & Carmeli, 2009)
	Recognition, Autonomy and Power: A Qualitative Retrospective Examination
Final Interview	• See Appendix 4 for interview questions*

Note: * Questions were developed by the authors of this book.

For the training efficacy component of the study, self-efficacy questions based on work-shop objectives were administered before and after each workshop. Another questionnaire assessing satisfaction and transferability was administered after each workshop as well. All instruments pertaining to training efficacy appear in Appendix 2.

For the demands, control, and stress component of the study, two different question-naires were administered: questionnaire A at time 0 and questionnaire B at times 1 and 2 (see Appendix 3). It contained, in addition to demographic questions (e.g., gender, age, language, nationality, profession, specialty, tenure in position, years of experience, level of education completed, experience with members of team), validated instruments measuring several constructs. A final retrospective interview was also conducted. Interview questions appear in Appendix 4.

Each of these instruments will be described in detail when each component of the study will be explained.

Sample

Projects

The type of projects that health care teams undertake can vary considerably in terms of duration, scope, and complexity. Each of the 11 teams included in this study had a differ-ent project, and each project presented its own challenges—nevertheless, all projects fell under one of two categories.

Project teams seeking to introduce a new mode of functioning or to substantially enhance the existing system (e.g., create and implement a structured collaborative approach) fell under "Changes and improvements in the service industry." Projects that sought more to disseminate best practices (e.g., a summary of accepted in-house best practices), were categorized into "Knowledge transfer and continuous education". As can be seen in Table 3.2, of the 11 projects included in the study, six under "Knowledge transfer and continuous edu-cation" and five were categorized under as "Changes in service delivery." It is noteworthy to mention that these categories are not mutually exclusive, as changes and improvements in service delivery involve some amount of knowledge transfer, while continuous education involves in some respect improvements to service delivery. In addition, knowledge transfer projects were often initial phases of larger change projects.

The scope of projects varied, as each team was asked to break down their project into phases required to reach their project goal, as well as the number of milestones mark-ing the progression or completion of each phase. Projects included in the study could be broken down into 5 phases on average, with a total of about 12.9 milestones per project ($SD = 4.72$). Some projects started later or lasted longer than expected and thus were still underway at the time of publication[1].

As will be discussed in Chapter 4, teams were shown how to create a simple project char-ter, scope statement (which we reproduced in Table 3.2), detailed planning, and risk manage-ment plan. Depending on each project, these varied in length, importance, and complexity.

---

[1]Measures of performance were worded so that the assessment was robust to this fact. See Appendix 2.

Table 3.2: Project Descriptions.

Project	Scope Statement*	Organization (Category)	Estimated planned duration	Estimated number of milestones
01	This project aims to create an online training program as well as workshops to perfect the reflexive approach and collaborative competencies of health care professionals. The goal is to improve the quality of care and collaborative work by December 2011. **	University (1)	17 months	N/A**
02	Faced with several interpersonal issues, this project consists of creating a training program on interprofessional collaboration for the entire radiology department, allowing for the development of a culture of collaborative practice that will benefit the patient, the personnel, as well as the health care institution.	Radiology Department (1)	12 months	11
03	Within the next six months, this project plans to create and implement an evaluative process and an integrated, more fluid intervention for adult psychiatric patients requiring specialized care for their cardio-metabolic pathologies.	Clinical Psychiatric Care Group (2)	6 months	8
04	This project aims to develop educational tools by April 2011 in order to equip teams with the resources necessary to complete projects pertaining to the improvement of collaborative practice and interprofessional learning for student-residents.	Administrative Group (1)	7 months	13
05	This project will improve a computerized reference tool to better equip interprofessional teams, as well as develop a user guide.	Geriatric Services (2)	8 months	11
06	This project consists of developing and implementing a collaborative interprofessional approach by June 2011 in order to improve patient care and effective teamwork, as well as promote this approach in the department.	Family Medicine Unit (2)	9 months	15
07	This project aims to create and implement a group training course by September 2011 in order to reorganize interprofessional clinical work, as well as increase the involvement of patients and their families in the management of their chronic kidney diseases.	Pre-Dialysis Clinic (1)	12 months	20
08	This project will create a training session by November 2011 which aims at enabling professionals to recognize drug-withdrawal symptoms in newborns, treat them interdisciplinarily and later transfer these competencies to other caretakers.	Neonatal Care Unit (1)	13 months	4
09	This project aims to develop and implement a structured collaborative approach for the interprofessional teams by September 2011, in order to improve client-care and attain treatment goals.	Family Medicine Unit (2)	9 months	18
10	Faced with the problem of patients, their families and support-staff misunderstanding the nature and processes of this project, the aim is to develop a user-guideline tool by March 2012, in order to reassure the user and his or her close ones of their future as well as support the internal and external staff involved in the program of long-term care.	Long-Term Care Unit (2)	13 months	16
11	This project plans to create great a new program by November 2011 in order to equip future graduates with the competencies required for their careers.	Faculty of Medicine (2)	9 months	13

Note: *Scope statements, estimated durations, and number of milestones were taken from teams' project charter following the first workshop.
   **This team did not provide a scope statement or milestones.
   Category 1: Knowledge transfer within teams and/or to patients and continuous education; Category 2: Changes and improvements in service delivery.

Teams and Team Members

Table 3.3 shows each project team's size. Project teams had an average of seven members $(SD = 2.14)$. All teams were comprised of health care practitioners from various professions, with some teams including administrative staff. The total number of participants across the 11 teams was 76 (72% women). The mean age of participants was 43.38 $(SD = 11.17)$ years old. The vast majority of participants were French-speaking $(N = 72;$ 94.7%) Canadians $(N = 69; 90.8\%)$. Participants had an average of 16.49 $(SD = 10.83)$ years of experience in their profession, and had held their current position an average of 5.65 years $(SD = 7.55)$. There were times at which a participant was not able to attend one of the three training sessions, or were unable to complete a questionnaire or interview because of scheduling conflicts.

In terms of acquaintance with other team members, 41.4% of participants reported working with their team members for the first time, 28.6% said they had worked a few times with some members of their team, 8.6% had worked a few times with most of the members of their team, 2.9% had worked frequently with some members of their team, 12.9% had worked frequently with most of their fellow team members, and 5.7% reported having worked frequently with all the members on their team. This distribution allowed for an interesting diversity in the familiarity of team members with each other, across groups.

In addition, of the total participants across all 11 teams, there were 11 different types of physicians (general practitioners, urologists, OB-GYNs, radiologists, surgeons, pediatric gastroenterologists, among others). The range of professions was equally vast: secretaries, nurses, social workers, occupational therapists, administrative assistants, magnetic resonance imaging technologists, medical student residents, research assistants, human resources support personnel, etc. It is apparent that inter-professional health care teams are

Table 3.3: Number of Team Members and Research Participants Across Research Phases.

Project Number	Team Size	QA*	Tr1	Tr2	QB$_1$	Tr3	QB$_2$	FI
01	5	5	5	5	4	5	3	3
02	8	8	7	6	9	8	6	6
03	5	5	5	3	**	**	4	1
04	8	8	8	8	7	6	7	5
05	7	6	7	7	6	7	6	6
06	6	5	5	5	5	4	4	4
07	6	8	6	7	8	8	5	5
08	6	6	6	6	5	5	4	4
09	9	9	7	7	5	6	5	7
10	8	6	6	6	6	6	4	4
11	5	5	5	5	3	4	2	5

Note: *QA: Questionnaire at time 0; QB : Questionnaires at times 1 or 2; Tr: Training sessions; FI: Final interviews;
** Data not collected because the project was terminated.

not limited to simply physicians and nurses, and among the teams included in this study there were nearly as many professions as there were participants. Therefore, a typical team could consist of a physician, pharmacist, a nutritionist, a research assistant, a program coordinator, and a nurse. With this variety of practitioners came a range in level of education. Unsurprisingly, nurses and physicians had a higher level of education;nevertheless, nearly half the participants had a university degree, and nearly a third held a master's degree or higher.

Finally, one aspect of this study was the variability in team membership as the projects progressed. As with any longitudinal studies, attrition took place. Also, not all team members could participate in all research activities. Although these issues complicated the research endeavor (i.e., it negatively affected statistical power), they are not unlike any other study conducted in natural settings.

Chapter 4

Training Efficacy

The Challenge

Projects are becoming mainstream in organizations (Pellegrinelli & Murray-Webster, 2011). Once limited to construction and engineering, project-based work is now spreading to a variety of sectors such as software, insurance, banking (Keegan, Turner, & Huemann, 2007), and education (Chiocchio & Lafrenière, 2009), and health care (Dwyer, Stanton, & Thiessen, 2004).

The health care sector has long recognized the necessity to work collaboratively across professions and disciplines (D'Amour et al., 2005). However, the shift is mainly occurring at the core business processes of the sector—where the aim is to improve health service delivery. The design and implementation of such endeavors (i.e., projects) is not discussed as thoroughly in the health care sector, despite their many challenges.

Although the need to acquire project management knowledge is somewhat recognized among hospital personnel, finding time to acquire it is a significant challenge for physicians, nurses, and other health professionals, as well as technicians and administrative personnel contemplating working on a project. In designing and delivering our project management training, we faced an important—yet ironic—challenge: even if people understand that ill-managed projects create re-work (Kerzner, 2003), that re-work adds to workload, and that increased workload fosters stress (Cooper, Dewe, & O'Driscoll, 2001), many health care workers are too busy to take time off "regular work" to acquire training that will alleviate these problems. In other words, they find it difficult to invest time now—even it will save them time and grief later.

Fundamental Criteria

This ironic challenge led us to design our training with the following four criteria outlined in Table 4.1.

Comprehensiveness

The first criterion pertains to the choice and combination of pertinent concepts, as well as the effectiveness with which the training is delivered. Let us first discuss the issue of choice. The project management literature offers a wealth of concepts, tools, and techniques that help improve projects' processes and outcome (cf. Kerzner, 2003). Although choosing

Table 4.1: Fundamental Criteria for the Design and Delivery of Effective Project Team Training in Health Care.

1.	Comprehensiveness. The training must be short, but comprehensive. Only the most fundamental concepts of interprofessional collaboration and project management must be identified and integrated seamlessly in a single short program.
2.	Specificity. The training must be specific to the project teams' current project. Consequently, tools and techniques must be relevant, usable in real-time, and easily transferable to any future projects team members would be involved in.
3.	Just-in-time. Training must be delivered on-site and just-in-time – that is, according to their project's planning and milestones.
4.	Relatedness. Training must be delivered by a tandem of trainers with diverse occupational backgrounds and they should be role models participants can identify with.

the very few that can capture the essence of project management is a tall order, our task was easier when taking into account the particularities of our target population.

A needs analysis and discussions in our team resulted in the following conclusions. We anticipated projects would likely be small, that is, take less about one year to complete, and consume only part-time human resources, and few financial resources. As a rule, participants would have no prior training in management of any sort, let alone project management. Although perceived as complex and unclear in relative terms by team members themselves—not surprisingly, given the lack of project management experience and knowledge—projects would be simple in absolute terms; they would have well defined goals and well defined solutions (i.e., type 1 projects, Turner, 2009, p. 22).

As Table 4.2 shows and the following sections will detail, what we believe are three core project management principles helped us choose training concepts and materials.

Characteristics of our target population and our core principles guided our choices, and facilitated the elimination of certain topics of "regular" project management training. For example, it was clear we needed to avoid in-depth presentations of matrix management, detailed analysis of process groups and all their inputs, multiple tools and techniques, and outputs. We did not adopt a strict engineering and/or construction approach with in-depth explanations of Project Evaluation and Review Technique (PERT) or Critical Path Method (CPM), for instance. We did not discuss procurement management and its many types of contracts. We did not elaborate on all the documents that can be created during a project.

Table 4.2: Core Project Management Principles.

1.	The team must learn to acquire at the beginning – and maintain throughout the life cycle of the project – a clear and shared understanding the desired outcome of the project and of the process that lead to it.
2.	Uncertainty, planning, and control are integral elements of project work. a. Project management in general helps reduce uncertainty, but does not eliminate it. Decision-making is ambiguous and results from analysis and trade-offs. b. Planning saves future re-work, re-planning as information is gathered is not a sign of failure. c. To control a project, a team must create an inward stream of interpretable information to ascertain the extent to which project phases and activities are successful and team members and stakeholders are satisfied.
3.	Team members must understand what drives them to engage in project tasks and activities as well as understand how to engage each other (i.e., the team) and external stakeholders so the project will succeed.

In addition to carefully choosing project management concepts—to which we will turn shortly—how they are combined to what the project management community qualifies as "soft" is another important issue. Our belief is that learning to be a better project team implies both better project management and better interprofessional collaboration. In fact, we view them as inextricably linked.

While the technical aspects of project management progressed in leaps and bounds over the last decades, developments of the behavioral system (Belout, 1998) contributing to project success did not enjoy the same rapid developments (Chiocchio, 2009). Furthermore, developments made in the "soft" fields themselves (i.e., organizational behavior, work and organizational psychology) during the same period were not necessarily integrated in the project management literature (Chiocchio, Messikomer, Hobbs, Allen, & Lamerson, 2011). Hence, while our challenge with project management concepts was to choose the most pertinent among a vast away of concepts, we sought to integrate updated "soft" components from the organizational behavior and work psychology literature.

For example, the project management literature insists that taking time to learn how to work together is important early in the project management life cycle (Turner, 2009). However, Tuckman's five-stage model of team development (Tuckman, 1965; Tuckman & Jensen, 1977) is not the most recent theory to explain how teams develop. Team compilation theory explains more thoroughly how individuals become a team by emphasizing transitions in team development from understanding tasks to understanding roles (Kozlowski, Gully, Nason, & Smith, 1999). Hence, we designed materials that discussed project management basics in parallel with the importance of defining which and how team members' formal and informal roles would benefit the project.

Similarly, project management is largely based on the understanding that project activities are organized in some logical way along a timeline. In parallel, organizing project activities necessarily involves matching activities with human resources. We therefore discussed activity identification, sequencing and duration estimation in parallel with self-determination theory (Deci, Connell, & Ryan, 1989; Gagné & Deci, 2005), a more useful framework than Malsow's (1943) hierarchy of needs theory (see Kanfer, Chen, & Pritchard, 2008, for a review). Self-determination theory provides a means to understand how to engage and motivate oneself, how to motivate others in the team, and how a team can influence stakeholders. Finally, monitoring and control are key features of project management (Kerzner, 2003) allowing projects to progress and adapt when required as they navigate through complexity.

Similarly, high performing teams are those that can adapt to complex environmental demands (Griffin et al., 2007; Kozlowski et al., 1999). Just as projects must integrate and analyze information to progress, teams must also acquire information on their internal dynamics, critically assess how they function, and adapt as required. This is why in parallel with training on monitoring and risk management, we also integrated reflexivity concepts (Schön, 1983) in the form of a multi-source feedback report designed as a monitoring device for individual and team behaviors (see Appendix 8).

With these remarks in mind we created three three-hour workshops designed to provide an adequate basis for project teams to acquire explicit knowledge and start experimenting with it during and between workshops in order to foster tacit knowledge. Loosely based on scaffolding

Table 4.3: Outline of Training Modules.

Workshop	Project Management Topics	Interprofessional Collaboration Topics	Workshop Outcome
1. Start your project	Project management basics and mandate clarification	Roles	Create project charter
2. Plan your project	Identify, sequence, and estimate duration of project activities	Motivation	Create detailed planning
3. Execute your project	Risk and change management	Individual and team feedback	Create risk management plan

techniques (Ausubel, 1968), each workshop aimed at providing foundations necessary for subsequent workshops, while also progressing from mostly instructor-driven and theoretical, to mostly to discussion-focused and applied. Table 4.3 shows the outline of each workshop.

Specificity

The second of the four criteria shown in Table 4.1 refers to specificity and the need for relevant and effective training techniques. According to Kolb's learning cycle (1984), explicit knowledge is transferable in two ways. First, trainers can transfer explicit knowledge in traditional ways if abstract concepts are properly codified and clearly communicated. Second, explicit knowledge becomes tacit if learners practice and test concepts communicated explicitly. Accordingly, we sought to capture the essence of the principles we outline in Table 4.1 by using templates as boundary objects.

A boundary object is an artifact that serves as an interface facilitating knowledge sharing and interactions in a multidisciplinary context (Chiocchio & Forgues, 2008). Instead of explaining why and how a particular concept is important, the apparent simple act of using a boundary object enables experiential learning as well as provides an opportunity to actually work and advance the project. Templates across all workshops were pre-filled with a running example of a typical health care service improvement project. After showing and briefly discussing a filled-in template, each team used the blank version to advance their project during the workshop, where trainers were on hand to help. Teams were instructed to continue on their own after the workshop and finish completing each template before the start of the next workshop. Trainers were on call to answer questions as required. The first exercise asked the team to fill a template of a project charter. The second exercise asked the team to create a detailed plan. The third exercise focused on creating a risk management plan. Although these exercises and templates may appear self-evident or simplistic to the experienced project manager, one must keep in mind our target audience—physicians, nurses, health technicians or administrative personnel, although well trained to address in their "regular" complex ongoing tasks and work processes, typically have no training in project management. These templates and exercises represent a significant increase of knowledge.

Just-in-Time

The third criteria for the design and delivery of an effective training in health care from Table 4.1 addresses on-site just-in-time delivery. Each workshop had to be delivered at the most convenient time for our target population. The main reason was to accommodate the fact that it is a very significant challenge to halt ongoing health care services to participate in training. Just-in-time also meant that workshops needed to be delivered for each team separately on their job site at times in the project life-cycle when each team deemed most relevant for their project. We, as researchers, did not impose timelines to the teams included in the study and minimized as much as possible the impact of our own schedule constraints. Indeed, our project was an *action-research project* (Goldebhar, LaMontagne, Katz, Heaney, & Landsbergis, 2001). This meant that both the training and the study components of our project were relevant and evidence-based in and of their own. However, when a trade-off needs to be made, action superseded research.

Relatedness

The fourth and last criterion in Table 4.1 addresses role modeling. We define role-modeling as a teaching strategy that entails enacting behaviors and subsequently meta-communicating on those behaviors in order to demonstrate their value in specific situations. Role modeling is rooted in concepts such as apprenticeship, situated learning, observational learning, and reflective practice (Kenny, Mann, & MacLeod, 2003) and is an effective means to convey attitudes and values (Weissmann, Branch, Gracey, Haidet, & Frankel, 2006). Because role modeling implies credibility on the part of trainers and facilitators, we made certain that workshop trainers and facilitators were seasoned experts in both interprofessional collaboration and project management. Furthermore, because facilitators were themselves from divergent professional disciplines and because learning is more effective if behaviors can be observed as well as practiced, facilitators made a conscious effort to be good role models and to "walk the talk" of interprofessional collaboration. Adding role modeling to our program's arsenal fostered trust and mutual respect that, in turn, helped team members engage in the workshop and work diligently on the project between workshops. Perhaps more importantly, because facilitators were candid about their own experience with the challenges of interprofessional collaboration, role-modeling also encouraged discussions on sensitive topics such team dynamics.

Design of Training Sessions and Materials

Workshop 1. Start Your Project

The first workshop aimed at setting foundations for teams' project and the other workshops. Its learning objectives were to foster the following behaviors:

1. Identify the main element that distinguishes project work from other forms of work.
2. Identify each element of the triple constraint.
3. Identify the types of decisions that occur at the beginning of a project and those that occur at the end.
4. Understand the difference between a formal role and an informal role.
5. Become aware of roles you can play on your team.
6. Start putting together your project charter.

The module started with basic definitions of teams and projects. A team is a group of individuals with a common goal and who are task interdependent (Hackman, 1987, 1990).

An efficient team must learn to manage these interdependencies (S. G. Cohen & Bailey, 1997). A project is a temporary organization used to create a unique product or a service (Turner & Müller, 2003). Temporariness and uniqueness combine so that a project must be progressively elaborated (Project Management Institute, 2008).

The next portion discussed how decision-making is affected by the way scope, time, costs, quality, and purpose (Turner, 2009) interact. We used Kerzner's (2003) iron triangle of time, cost and quality as a visual support, but discussions and examples on decision-making and trade-offs took footing on all five constraints. This was followed by a discussion on project process groups (i.e., initiating, planning, executing, controlling, closing) (Project Management Institute, 2008), how they can represent a part or the entire project, and how planning, executing, and controlling can be construed as a feedback loop. As a final component of project management basics, the workshop explained how the cost of making changes to the project increases as the project progresses.

The workshop then proceeded with definitions of formal and informal roles. In general, role behaviors are "recurring actions of an individual, appropriately interrelated with the repetitive activities of others so as to yield a predictable outcome" (Katz & Kahn, 1978, p. 189). Hence, repetitive patterns create a forum for people to play their part as well as a structure shaping others' expectations. Hence, we defined a formal role as rooted in task work and occurring as a function of a group's norms and expectations determined by the interaction of hierarchy, profession, and status within the team. An informal role is related more directly to personality and individual preferences (Katz & Kahn, 1978) than to task work and can include roles such as peacemaker and the scapegoat (Farrell, Schmitt, & Heinemann, 2001). Another role that is often informal is that of devil's advocate. A devil's advocate purposefully engages in counterarguments in order to improve on the decision-making process (Schwenk & Valacich, 1994).

Because conflicts are "perceived incompatibilities or discrepant views" (Jehn & Bendersky, 2003, p. 189) our workshop included a discussion of each other's perceptions of team norms, expectations, and formal and informal roles. This effort to make explicit what is usually only implicit had two objectives. First, it was designed to prevent potential conflicts based on false or unrealistic expectations. Second, an explicit discussion on team norms and role expectations aimed at creating clear, relevant, and realistic expectations on which to build trust.

The main component of workshop 1 was an exercise on creating a simple project charter (Appendix 5). The exercise is designed not only to create an important document and communication tool, but to foster a clear shared mental model of the project's outcome and process. A shared mental model consists of organized knowledge structures that shape interactions and help teams adapt to difficult and changing conditions (Mathieu, Heffner, Goodwin, Salas, & Cannon-Bowers, 2000). In addition to including names and coordinates of all team members; describing team members' formal and informal roles; identifying stakeholders, their expectations; and how these expectations will be met, and a bigpicture view of major phases and milestones, the charter asked teams to formally and briefly describe the team's mandate and project objective.

Teams followed a simple structure to craft a short paragraph that answered the following questions:

- What is (are) the problem(s) the project aims at addressing?
- What is the name of the project?
- What is the goal of the project? (i.e., "aims at" + infinitive action verb)
- What is the service or product of the project?
- How will the project outcome solve the problems?
- When will it be delivered?

Teams were then instructed to assemble the answers to these deceivingly simple questions into a short and structured paragraph we designated as the scope statement (All teams' scope statements appear in Table 3.2). Not all teams were equally successful at capturing all the elements of a short comprehensive scope statement. Although there were other elements to the exercise (see Appendix 5), one key component was identifying internal and external stakeholders, pinpointing their needs and requirements, and anticipating measures that will inform the team and the stakeholders if and to what extent their requirements will be met.

Workshop 2. Plan the Project

The second workshop started with an open discussion of workshop 1 topics, feedback and Q&As on the team's completed project charter, and challenges they had to overcome to progress on their project between both workshops. This discussion served as a good introduction to workshop 2's learning objectives which were to encourage team members to:

1. Invest yourself in the project, despite the constraints.
2. Negotiate your expectations with other teammates.
3. Interact with your teammates to maximize the contribution of each.
4. Understand your involvement and that of others in each of the tasks of the project.
5. Identify tasks that are critical to the project.
6. Estimate the duration of a group of dependent tasks.
7. Begin the detailed plan of your project.

The first part of the workshop discussed motivation. Our training focused on self-determination theory (Gagné & Deci, 2005). Self-determination theory explains why people engage in specific behaviors and describes 6 types of motivation from amotivation (i.e., not knowing why we carry out behaviors) to intrinsic motivation (i.e., carrying out tasks because they are pleasurable). Most importantly, the theory distinguishes between four types of extrinsic motivation that vary from controlled by external and environmental factors (e.g., benefits, how others judge our performance) to autonomous factors (e.g., because we recognize ourselves in the values emanating from the meaning of our behaviors, because we believe certain behaviors are important). Knowing why team members engage (or not) in project tasks and why stakeholders engage (or not) in what is necessary for the project to succeed was shown as a mechanism by which teams members could self-motivate, motivate each other, and influence others outside of the team.

How people can engage in project tasks tied in well into the next topic of the workshop: planning and allocating resources to project activities. Here teams were told that the apparently simple task of identifying all project activities, ordering them in a temporal sequence, placing them in a calendar, estimating their duration, and determining "who" will be doing "what" was, in fact, quite difficult. Most importantly, they were told that it is normal to find it difficult, but that trying to answer these questions helps identifying "unknowns" and bring them on the "knowns" side of the project management equation, and helps to strengthen a shared mental model of the project and its process as well. After additional remarks on activity dependency and the advantages of thinking of pessimistic, realistic, and optimistic activity duration estimates, the workshop proceeded with its main exercise.

A template of an "activity form" was used as a boundary object (see Appendix 6). As with other templates we used, the form is deceivingly simple. Each form asks who will do what project activity for how long, what roles team members and other key people will play to ensure the success of the activity, and what metric, measure, or information will be used to assess the success of the activity. The form also forced team members to assess if each activity was critical, and if so, why and how. In spite of its apparent simplicity, using this simple technique helped strengthen project management principles into a concrete activity. It also created a forum for interprofessional discussions that unearthed inadequacies of what came out of the previous workshop (for example, this step usually required teams to update their project charter). One interesting point was that initially, most team members thought that having to improve on the project chapter was a sign of failure. Trainers were on hand to participate in discussions and explain that sort of work is, in fact, part of project management and progressive elaboration. Discussions among team members also prepared them well for issues they were going to address in the next workshop: risk management.

Workshop 3. Execute your Project.

The third and last workshop started with an open discussion of the previous workshop's topics and the detailed planning teams did in between the second and third workshops. By that time, all teams had a very clear understanding of their project outcome and processes. This was a perfect time to tackle the following behaviors/learning objectives:

1. Identify risks to the project.
2. Propose solutions to manage risks.
3. Analyze the relevance of changes to the project.
4. Establish individual goals that aim to improve the efficiency of the team.
5. Take measures to improve the efficiency of the team.

Teams were told that, by and large, executing the project activities is not the most difficult component of project management. Execution refers to their individual competencies and expertise and as such is the most well-known aspect of the project. The challenge to executing a project is dealing with unforeseen events and changes to the plan. It is an art to know when to stick to the plan and adopt a traditional view of project management and when it is better to adopt an agile perspective and thrive on opportunities and changes brought in because of the very nature of projects (i.e., progressive elaboration) (Wysocki, 2009).

To assess project risks in an inexperienced interprofessional project team, it is important all team members have a voice in identifying risks, analyzing their potential likeliness and impact, and participate in planning for control or preventive measures. While unstructured discussions offer the potential for success in such tasks, they also reinforce situations where status, experience, or personal preferences in team discussions prevent all team members from sharing their views. Social and work psychology largely contributed to understand the dynamics of these phenomena (Choi & Kim, 1999). To avoid such pitfalls, the workshop discussed how teams must learn to disentangle individual analysis from group discussions and consensus making, and how to clearly separate risk identification from discussions of solutions to risks.

The workshop proceeded with a risk identification and risk management planning exercise (see Appendix 7). Once risks were identified and rated for likelihood and impact through individual analysis and group discussions, the exercise guided teams to consider the most important risks as preventable, controllable, and/or acceptable (Project Management Institute, 2008). Preventing a risk means that the team operates at the source of the risk to reduce its probability. Controlling a risk means that the team is taking steps to reduce the negative consequences of the risk. Accepting a risk means that the team is aware of the existence of the risk, but chooses not to take any specific measures to control it.

The workshop then proceeded to distribute personalized multi-source feedback reports. The feedback report showed how a team member rated himself/herself compared to the rest of the team and how his/her team compared to all other teams (see Appendix 8).

The report was based on data gathered through the research process using validated questionnaires measuring individual and team dynamics-relevant constructs. Topics included informational role self-efficacy(Chiocchio, Dubé, et al., 2012), project commitment (Hoegl et al., 2004), and Intra-team trust (Simons & Peterson, 2000). How team members support each other was also part of the feedback report (Cutrona & Russell, 1987). The interdisciplinary collaboration questionnaire (Vinokur-Kaplan, 1995) also served that purpose. Finally conflict types (Jehn & Mannix, 2001) and conflict management strategies (De Dreu et al., 2001) were showcased. Conflict management strategies (i.e., avoiding, forcing, compromising, yielding, and problem solving) are based on the dual concern theory (Pruitt & Rubin, 1986).

In accordance with goal-setting theory (Locke & Latham, 2002, 1990), team members were shown how to examine their report and extract information to craft one or two individual development goals that were difficult, but achievable and measurable. Furthermore, we suggested they discuss one individual goal with others on the team and further suggested each individual adopt complementary behaviors to help the others achieve their goals. Teams could also set team-level goals.

The Impact of Training: Main Hypotheses

Training is supposed to impact participants in relevant ways. Kirkpatrick (1996) suggests four levels of training efficacy. First, participants should feel satisfied with the training received. Second, the training should transfer knowledge and skills (which, said differently, means that participants should experience a gain in these areas). Third, this gain should translate into new behaviors. Fourth, the training and by extension, the new behaviors, should impact work.

Going back to the objectives of this book, we hypothesized the following:

- Hy 4.1 – Participants will be satisfied with the workshops.
- Hy 4.2 – Participants will report an increase in transferred knowledge and skills.
- Hy 4.3 – Measures of training efficacy will be positively related to job demands.
- Hy 4.4 – Measures of training efficacy will be positively related to job control.
- Hy 4.5 – Measures of training efficacy will be negatively related to stress.
- Hy 4.6 – Measures of training efficacy will be positively related to collaborative behaviors.
- Hy 4.7 – Measures of training efficacy will be negatively related to manifestations of conflict.
- Hy 4.8 – Measures of training efficacy will be positively related to performance behaviors.
- Hy 4.9 – Measures of training efficacy will be positively related to project performance.

The first two hypotheses correspond to Kirkpatrick's (1996) first two levels. Hypothesis 4.3 embodies his third and fourth levels.

Methods

Process

Our study process and timing of our measures are detailed in Figure 1 and Table 3.1.

Measures of Training Efficacy

We used individual self-reported questionnaires to assess training efficacy. All questionnaires appear in Appendix 2. One questionnaire was administered immediately before each workshop and another was administered immediately after each workshop. Using principles outlined by Bandura (2006) regarding self-efficacy, we asked participants to rate on a scale from 0% to 100% the confidence with which they believed they could carry out a list of clearly outlined behaviors. These behaviors were actually the objectives for each workshop as discussed earlier in this chapter. Once all pre- and post-workshop ratings were collected, we subtracted post-workshop ratings from pre-workshop ratings and to create an average score difference over all objectives for each participant. Conceptually, the resulting index is the mean gain in self-efficacy beliefs each participant experienced as a function of each workshop. Workshop objectives were related either to human factors or to project management factors. Overall, this procedure yielded two self-efficacy gain scores per participant per workshop.

In addition to self-efficacy ratings drawn from workshop objectives, the post-workshop questionnaire also had a 15-item scale measuring training efficacy adapted by Beaulieu (in progress) from works of Rivard (2006) and Saks and Haccoun (2010). These items had to be answered using an agreement response format (i.e., 1 = disagree completely, 5 = agree completely). Items were grouped under two dimensions. First, satisfaction regarding reactions to and contentment with the workshop was assessed with 15 items (e.g., *The workshop leaders provided ample relevant examples*). Second, transferability of knowledge acquired during the workshop was assessed with five items (e.g., *The knowledge acquired during the workshops can be directly applied to my job*). Both dimensions yielded high internal consistency.

Alpha coefficients for satisfaction for the three workshops were .87, .93, and .92 respectively. Similarly, transferability showed high internal consistency with α = .82, .87, and .87 for the three workshops.

Measures Onto which Training Efficacy are Assessed

Job demands, job control, and stress

Job demands refers to psychological stressors present in the work environment, such as high time pressure and workload, role conflicts, and physical and emotional demands (Karasek, 1979). We measured job demands with Bosma et al.'s (1997) four-item questionnaire (e.g., *I must work very intensely*). Participants had to estimate the frequency with which they performed the behaviors using a five-point scale (1 = Never or almost never; 5 = Very often). Once item 3 was removed at both times for lack of variance, internal consistency indices in our sample for this variable were α = .79 and .77 at times 1 and 2.

Job control refers to the extent to which a person is capable of controlling their tasks and general work activity (Häusser, Mojzisch, Niesel, & Schulz-Hardt, 2010). We measured job control items from Bosma et al.'s (1997) questionnaire. The questionnaire measure two dimensions of job control: decision authority (nine items; e.g., *I have a choice in deciding what I do at work*) and skill discretion (6 items; e.g., *My job provides me with a variety of interesting things to do*). Participants had to estimate the frequency with which they performed the behaviors using a five-point scale (1 = Never or almost never; 5 = Very often). Internal consistency indices in our sample for this variable were α = .82 and .70 at time 1, and .85 and .76 at time 2.

Perceived stress refers to the degree to which situations in one's life are appraised as stressful (S. Cohen et al., 1983) . Ten of the 14 items from the Perceived Stress Scale developed by these authors were used to measure the variable (e.g., *In the last month, how often have you felt that you were on top of things?*). Participants had to estimate the frequency with which they performed the behaviors using a five-point scale (1 = Never or almost never; 5 = Very often). Internal consistency indices in our sample for this variable were α = .75 and .84 at times 1 and 2.

Collaboration

Collaborative refers to the interplay of situation-appropriate uses of four interrelated processes (Chiocchio, Grenier, et al., 2012): teamwork communication (information exchange), synchronicity (on time and in accordance with each others' tasks), explicit coordination ("who" does "what" "when") and implicit coordination (anticipation of each others' needs and adaptation without explicit coordination). We measured collaborative work with Chiocchio et al's (2012) 14-item questionnaire. The questionnaire measures the four dimensions of collaboration: Teamwork communication (e.g., *My teammates and I share knowledge that promotes work progress)*, synchronicity (e.g., *My teammates and I carry out our tasks at the appropriate moment)*, explicit coordination (e.g., *My teammates and I discuss work deadlines with each other)*, and implicit coordination (e.g., *My teammates and I can foresee each others' needs without having to express them)*. Participants had to estimate the frequency with which they performed the behaviors using a five-point scale (1 = Never or almost never; 5 = Very often). At time 1, internal consistency indices in our sample were α=93, .89, .93, and .88 for these dimensions, respectively. At time 2, indices were α = 93, .92, .93, and .85.

Interdisciplinary collaboration refers to "an effective interpersonal process that facilitates the achievement of goals that cannot be reached when individual professionals act on their own" (Bronstein, 2003, p. 299). We measured interdisciplinary collaboration with Vinokur-Kaplan's (1995) 10-item questionnaire (e.g., *Exposure to the role of other disciplines has increased my awareness of their contribution*). Participants had to answer using a five-point scale (1 = Strongly disagree; 5 = Strongly agree). Internal consistency indices in our sample for this variable were $\alpha = .82$ at time 1 and .76 at time 2.

Conflict

Conflict is an awareness on the part of the parties involved of discrepancies, incompatible wishes, or irreconcilable desires and what people do because of them (Chiocchio, Forgues, Paradis, & Iordanova, 2011). We measured conflicts with Jehn & Mannix's (2001) nine-item questionnaire, but adapted to address frequency (i.e., 1 = Never or almost never; 5 = Very often) as suggested by De Dreu and Van Vianen (2001). The questionnaire measured three dimensions of conflict: Relationship conflict (three items; e.g., *How frequently does your team experience manifestations of anger?*), task conflict (three items; e.g., *How frequently does your team experience disagreements about the task to accomplish?*), and process conflict (three items; e.g., *How frequently does your team experience disagreements about resource allocation?*). At time 1, internal consistency indices in our sample were $\alpha = .76$, .69, and .70 for these dimensions, respectively. At time 2, they were $\alpha = .79$, .69, and .66.

Behavioral performance

Performance is a multilevel construct: individual, team, and project. Individual performance refers to individuals' behaviors contributing to individual effectiveness, while team member performance refers to individuals' behaviors contributing to team effectiveness (Griffin et al., 2007; Motowidlo, 2003). Each of these levels of performance is divided into three work role behaviors: proficiency (fulfillment of the prescribed requirements of the role), adaptivity (coping with, responding to, and supporting change) and proactivity (initiating change). Consequently, we measured performance with 18 of the 27 items of Griffin et. al.'s (2007) questionnaire: individual task proficiency (e.g., *I carried out the core parts of my job well)*, individual task adaptivity (e.g., *I adapted well to changes in core tasks)*, individual task proactivity (e.g., *I come up with ideas to improve the way in which my core tasks are done)*, team member proficiency (e.g., *I coordinated my work with others)*, team member adaptivity (e.g., *I dealt effectively with changes affecting my team)*, team member proactivity (e.g., *I Improved the way my team does things)*. Participants had to estimate the frequency with which they performed the behaviors using a five-point scale (1 = Never or almost never; 5 = Very often). At time 1, internal consistency indices in our sample were $\alpha = 90$, .92, .93, .87, .87, and .93 for these dimensions, respectively. At time 2, indices were $\alpha = 92$, .90, .94, .87, .89, and .94.

Project performance

Project performance refers to the extent to which a project is carried out on time, within budget, and satisfying client/customer requirements (Kerzner, 2003). Regular assessment of a project refers to the monitoring of defined activities to ensure that the project objectives are achieved (Stratman & Roth, 2002). We measured regular assessment of project with Stratman & Roth's (2002) questionnaire (e.g., *We constantly review our project capabilities against strategic goals*). Participants had to answer using a five-point scale (1 = Strongly disagree; 5 = Strongly agree). Internal consistency indices in our sample for this variable was α = .91 at time 1. At time 2, internal consistency was α = .92.

We also measured project performance with Gelbard & Carmeli's (1998) 10-item questionnaire. The questionnaire measured two dimensions of project performance: Budgetary and time performance (six items; e.g., *So far, this project didn't have budget overrun*) and functionality performance (four items; e.g., *So far, all project specifications were attained*). Participants had to answer using a five-point scale (1 = Strongly disagree; 5 = Strongly agree). At time 1, internal consistency indices in our sample were α = .66, and .86 for these dimensions, respectively. These indices became α = .75, and .88 at time 2.

Results
Self-efficacy, Satisfaction, and Transferability

Table 4.4 shows results pertinent to Hypotheses 4.1 and 4.2. Mean gains in self-efficacy regarding behaviors related to human factors and project management are positive, which points to an increase in self-efficacy for all three workshops. Means regarding satisfaction for workshops 1, 2, and 3 vary are very positive, approaching complete agreement. The same is true for transferability.

Table 4.4: Descriptive Statistics and Intercorrelations of Training Efficacy Measures.

	M (SD)	A	B	C	D	E	F	G	H	I	J	K	L
A. W1 – Human Factors	21.59 (18.84)	--											
B. W1 – Project Management	39.02 (22.33)	.67***	--										
C. W1 – Satisfaction	4.56 (0.30)	.12	.05	--									
D. W1 – Transferability	4.44 (0.49)	.23*	.21*	.56***	--								
E. W2 – Human Factors	5.14 (8.27)	.24*	.14	.08	.14	--							
F. W2 – Project Management	11.71 (8.66)	.14	.14	.00	.05	.51***	--						
G. W2 – Satisfaction	4.48 (0.44)	.12	.21	.16	.12	.13	.23	--					
H. W2 – Transferability‡	4.41 (0.54)	-.04	.03	.02	.22	.18	.34**	.69***	--				
I. W3 – Human Factors	19.00 (14.76)	.21	.04	.03	.08	.23	.30**	-.06	-.06	--			
J. W3 – Project Management	22.09 (14.51)	.17	.07	-.07	.07	.32**	.29**	-.08	-.16	.73***	--		
K. W3 – Satisfaction‡	4.54 (0.35)	-.15	.03	.41**	.21	.07	.21	.49***	.40***	.05	.08	--	
L. W3 – Transferability‡	4.49 (0.45)	-.06	-.12	.30**	.28*	.07	.14	.56***	.53**	.01	-.10	.70***	--

Note: * $p < .1$; ** $p < .05$; *** $p < .01$.
  N = 33 to 63
  ‡ Correlations are performed on squared transformation due to the skewness of the distribution (Tabachnick & Fidell, 2007).

Correlations between training efficacy measures tend to show consistency between self-efficacy gains and between satisfaction and transferability. Furthermore, self-efficacy gains, satisfaction and transferability early in the training program (i.e., W1) tend to relate positively to later phases of the program (i.e., W2 and W3). In addition to strong support for Hypotheses 4.1 and 4.2, these trends suggest a logic to the training program as well as to overall benefits.

However, consistent with Kirkpatrick's (1996) four levels of training efficacy, a training program should not only impact satisfaction, transferability, and peoples' capability to act (in our case, self-efficacy gains), it should also impact behaviors once people leave the workshop.

Job Demands, Control, and Perceived Stress

Table 4.5 shows the relationships between training efficacy measures and self-reports of job demands, job control, and stress.

Table 4.5 shows that not many correlations are statistically significant. Nonetheless, satisfaction with workshop 1 is statistically related to job demands at Time 1 so that as satisfaction increases, so does perceptions of job demands (i.e., $r = .32$). A similar trend is

Table 4.5: Correlations Between Measures of Training Efficacy and Job stress, Demands, and Control.

	1	2	3	4	5	6	7	8
W1 – Human Factors	-.13	.19	-.18	-.08	-.18	.09	-.13	.03
W1 – Project Management	.01	.04	.01	-.04	.07	.11	.07	.08
W1 – Satisfaction	.32**	-.13	.07	-.003	.16	.02	.02	-.12
W1 – Transferability	.08	.11	.13	-.12	.11	.23	.21	-.28*
W2 – Human Factors	-.15	-.06	-.10	.29**	-.05	.02	-.01	.11
W2 – Project Management	-.06	-.03	-.14	.16	-.21	-.14	-.04	.08
W2 – Satisfaction	.03	-.09	.01	-.03	-.01	-.12	-.002	-.05
W2 – Transferability	.16	-.06	-.16	.06	-.01	-.22	.03	-.08
W3 – Human Factors					-.08	-.02	-.09	.09
W3 – Project Management					-.13	.16	-.05	-.03
W3 – Satisfaction					.29*	-.21	.03	-.11
W3 – Transferability					.14	-.05	-.01	-.35**

Note: 1 = T1 Job demands; 2 = T1 Control decision authority; 3 = T1 Control skill discretion; 4 = T1 Perceived stress; 5 = T2 Job demands; 6 = T2 Control decision authority; 7 = T2 Control skill discretion; 8 = T2 Perceived stress.
* $p < .1$; ** $p < .05$; *** $p < .01$.
N = 16 to 63

seen between self-efficacy gains for human factors regarding workshop 2 and stress at time 1 (i.e., $r = .29$). Satisfaction with workshop 3 is positively related with jobs demands at time 2 (i.e., $r = .29$). Finally transferability at workshop 1 is negatively related to perceived stress at time 2 (i.e., $r = -.29$) and transferability at workshop 1 is negatively related to perceived stress at time 2 as well (i.e., $r = -.35$). In these last cases, increases in transferability of training tend to reduce self reports of stress weeks later.

Collaboration

Table 4.6 depicts results regarding the impact of the training program on collaborative behaviors.

Table 4.6 shows interesting trends. Gains in self-efficacy for human factors did not impact collaborative behaviors in later phases of the project. Gains in project management self-efficacy for workshop 1 impacted collaboration at time 1, with correlations ranging from .24 to .33 with teamwork communication, synchrony, and explicit coordination. Measures of satisfaction at workshop 1 affected teamwork communication, synchrony, and explicit coordination but later in the project (i.e., time 2) with correlations ranging from .28 to .43. Participants' satisfaction with workshop 2 affected all but one components of collaboration at time 1 with correlations between .29 and .50. Finally, transferability of

Table 4.6: Correlations Between Measures of Training Efficacy and Collaboration.

	1	2	3	4	5	6	7	8	9	10
W1 – Human Factors	.05	.11	.00	.14	-.03	-.02	-.00	-.18	.02	.00
W1 – Project Management	.33**	.27*	.24*	.19	-.01	.10	-.04	-.12	-.02	-.20
W1 – Satisfaction	.02	.00	.15	.14	.23	.43**	.38**	.28*	.25	.25
W1 – Transferability	.04	.05	.14	.11	.01	.16	.18	.07	.10	.04
W2 – Human Factors	.09	.17	.13	.21	.09	.06	.12	.06	.06	.18
W2 – Project Management	-.05	.00	.05	.01	.03	.04	.05	-.03	-.05	-.06
W2 – Satisfaction	.29*	.31*	.30*	.18	.50**	.20	.03	.12	.09	.25
W2 – Transferability	.21	.17	.21	.16	.14	.26	.17	.32*	.22	.29
W3 – Human Factors						-.14	-.10	-.15	-.19	-.11
W3 – Project Management						-.10	-.06	-.18	-.12	-.29
W3 – Satisfaction						.16	.09	.13	.08	.08
W3 – Transferability						.05	-.04	.00	-.02	-.09

Note: 1 = T1 Teamwork communication, 2 = T1 Synchrony, 3 = T1 Explicit coordination, 4 = T1 Implicit coordination, 5 = T1 Interprofessional, 6 = T2 Teamwork communication, 7 = T2 Synchrony, 8 = T2 Explicit coordination, 9 = T2 Implicit coordination, 10 = T2 Interprofessional.
* $p < .1$; ** $p < .05$; *** $p < .01$.
N = 16 to 63

knowledge and skills discussed at workshop 2 impacted self-reported explicit coordination ($r = .32$) at time 2. Hence, while training efficacy of workshop 3 did not seem to exert an effect on collaboration later in the projects' life cycle, many components of collaboration seem to have been affected by various measures of training efficacy for workshops 1 and 2. We conclude with moderate support of the impact of our training program on collaboration.

Conflict

Table 4.7 now turns to the issue of conflict. We hypothesized that our training program would reduce conflict behaviors.

As expected, all significant correlations are negative. In other words, increases in training efficacy reduced participants' self-report of conflict behaviors. Satisfaction with workshops 1 ($r = -.40$) was negatively related to process conflict at time 1. Human factors for workshop 3 were negatively related to relationship ($r = -.42$) and process ($r = -.48$) conflict at time 2. Project management factors for workshop 3 were negatively related to all conflict measures at time 2 (relationship: $r = -.38$; task: $r = -.37$; process: $r = -.42$). Moreover, statistically significant human factor correlations were stronger than project

Table 4.7: Correlations Between Measures of Training Efficacy and Conflict.

	1	2	3	4	5	6
W1 – Human Factors	.03	-.10	.02	-.21	-.06	-.15
W1 – Project Management	.05	-.08	.03	-.15	-.18	-.06
W1 – Satisfaction	.03	-.12	-.40***	.11	-.11	-.21
W1 – Transferability	-.08	.03	-.12	-.30*	-.05	-.18
W2 – Human Factors	.01	-.13	.17	-.17	-.25	-.27
W2 – Project Management	-.03	.10	.23	-.21	-.01	.03
W2 – Satisfaction	.05	-.09	-.37**	-.22	-.14	-.21
W2 – Transferability	.07	-.01	-.07	-.26	.16	-.04
W3 – Human Factors				-.42**	-.26	-.48***
W3 – Project Management				-.38**	-.37**	-.42**
W3 – Satisfaction				-.09	.02	-.25
W3 – Transferability				.02	.06	-.02

Note: 1 = T1 Relationship conflict; 2 = T1 Task conflict, 3 = T1 Process conflict; 4 = T2 Relationship conflict; 5 = T2 Task conflict, 6 = T2 Process conflict.
* $p < .1$; ** $p < .05$; *** $p < .01$.
N = 16 to 63

management correlations. Because projects in later phase tended to be more hectic, and because workshop 3 discussed individuals' and the team's feedback reports–information for which was based on data from previous phases of the project (see Appendix 8)—we believe it is particularly interesting that self-efficacy gains in human factors and project management for workshop 3 show such striking results regarding conflict measures taken many weeks later. These results show moderate support for Hypothesis 4.7.

Performance

Behavioral performance

We now turn to behavioral performance (Table 4.8). Recall that these measures focused on what participants did to assert behaviors indicative of their own proficiency, adaptability and proactivity. Recall also that these measures focused on what participants contributed to the teams' capability to perform its task, adapt, and be proactive.

Surprisingly, all but one correlation are statistically significant: transferability of workshop 2 was significantly related to individual proactivity at time 2 ($r = .52$). This set of results does not permit us to conclude favorably on the training efficacy to influence performance behaviors.

Table 4.8: Correlations Between Measures of Training Efficacy and Performance Behaviors.

	1	2	3	4	5	6	7	8	9	10	11	12
W1 – Human Factors	.02	-.06	-.02	.00	-.07	-.11	-.08	-.17	-.19	-.12	.03	-.05
W1 – Project Management	.11	.12	.11	.17	.08	.06	.06	-.03	-.09	.08	-.03	-.12
W1 – Satisfaction	.07	.13	.14	-.04	.05	.14	.30	.29	.22	.28	.25	.27
W1 – Transferability	-.02	-.02	.00	-.07	.03	.03	.07	.01	-.02	.13	.02	.03
W2 – Human Factors	.00	-.01	-.06	-.01	-.01	.00	.09	.09	.03	.02	.08	.03
W2 – Project Management	-.28	-.18	-.13	-.19	-.11	-.09	.01	.10	.17	.06	.04	-.05
W2 – Satisfaction	.18	.18	.17	.22	.20	.11	.12	.11	.34	.12	.17	.01
W2 – Transferability	.00	-.04	.02	-.05	.03	.05	.19	.26	.52**	.21	.29	.14
W3 – Human Factors							-.28	-.27	-.26	-.30	-.22	-.26
W3 – Project Management							-.16	-.15	-.22	-.14	-.16	-.23
W3 – Satisfaction							.02	-.04	.20	-.04	.07	-.07
W3 – Transferability							.09	.02	.24	.06	.04	-.10

Note: 1 = T1 Individual taskwork; 2 = T1 individual adaptability, 3 = T1 individual proactivity; 4 = T1 Team taskwork; 5 = T1 Team adaptability, 6 = T1 Team proactivity; 7 = T2 Individual taskwork; 8 = T2 individual adaptability, 9 = T2 individual proactivity; 10 = T2 Team taskwork; 11 = T2 Team adaptability, 12 = T2 Team proactivity.
* $p < .1$; ** $p < .05$; *** $p < .01$.
$N = 16$ to 63

Project performance

Another important aspect of performance is project performance. Table 4.9 showcases the extent to which the efficacy of our program impacted individual accounts of each participant's project success.

Satisfaction with workshops 1 was significantly and positively related to budgetary and time performance at times 1 ($r = .28$) and 2 ($r = .44$), and satisfaction with workshop 2 was positively related to budgetary and time performance at time 1 ($r = .30$). All other correlations were non-significant. This set of results is not strikingly convincing of the training impact on project performance.

Results Summary and Preliminary Discussion

We hypothesized that the training efficacy of our program would be detected by having participants satisfied, by ensuring participants would report an increase in transferred knowledge and skills. We also suggested our program would be effective if participants translate self-efficacy gains into behaviors that will, in turn, increase their perceptions of job demands and of job control, decrease their levels of perceived stress, increase the frequency of collaborative

Table 4.9: Correlations Between Measures of Training Efficacy and Project Performance.

	1	2	3	4	5	6
W1 – Human Factors	-.02	.01	-.06	-.06	-.02	-.02
W1 – Project Management	.13	.21	.08	-.19	-.11	-.16
W1 – Satisfaction	.28*	-.00	-.01	.44***	.20	.05
W1 – Transferability	.12	-.01	.02	.19	.01	-.01
W2 – Human Factors	-.05	.11	-.14	.01	.02	-.04
W2 – Project Management	-.21	-.09	-.24	.10	-.23	-.10
W2 – Satisfaction	.30*	.16	.15	-.22	-.22	-.02
W2 – Transferability	.08	.04	.03	-.22	-.19	.29
W3 – Human Factors				-.08	-.19	-.22
W3 – Project Management				.04	.02	-.18
W3 – Satisfaction				.01	-.19	-.01
W3 – Transferability				.01	-.17	-.04

Note: 1 = T1 Budget and Time; 2 = T1 Functional; 3 = T1 Regular Assessment of Project;
4 = T2 Budget and Time; 5 = T2 Functional; 6 = T2 Regular Assessment of Projects.
$* p < .1$; $** p < .05$; $*** p < .01$.
$N = 16$ to 63

Table 4.10: Synthesis of Results for Training Efficacy.

Hypothesis		Level of Support
4.1	Participants will be satisfied with the workshops.	Strong support
4.2	Participants will report an increase in transferred knowledge and skills.	Strong support
4.3	Measures of training efficacy will be positively related to job demands.	Week to moderate
4.4	Measures of training efficacy will be positively related to job control.	No support
4.5	Measures of training efficacy will be negatively related to stress.	Mixed support
4.6	Measures of training efficacy will be positively related to collaborative behaviors.	Moderate support
4.7	Measures of training efficacy will be negatively related to manifestations of conflict.	Moderate support
4.8	Measures of training efficacy will be positively related to performance behaviors.	Not supported
4.9	Measures of training efficacy will be positively related to project performance.	Not supported

behaviors, decrease the frequency of conflict their behaviors, increase performance behaviors, and increase perceptions of project performance. Table 4.10 summarizes our results.

Some major trends regarding the efficacy of the training program merit attention. Our study showed that self-efficacy mean gain scores for all workshops are positive, which suggests participants felt an increase in capability beliefs after each workshop. Satisfaction and transferability measures did not suffer the same problem (i.e., difference score), since the score itself was used throughout. On average, participants were very much in agreement that the training was satisfactory and that valuable knowledge and skill were transferred.

As anticipated, many measures of training efficacy were correlated with self-reported measures so that increases in training efficacy appeared to have improved many important aspects of individual, team and project issues. This is the case with some stress measures, many components of collaboration and almost all measures of conflict.

Some measures of training efficacy seem to have worsened perceptions of job demands, job control, and stress. This phenomena occurred mostly at early phases (i.e., workshops 1 and 2 and time 1). Examining impacts at later phases (i.e., time 2) suggested a positive effect of training efficacy(i.e,. increases in training efficacy are negatively related to stress). It is possible that awakening health care workers to the challenges of interprofessional collaboration in the context of project management might have created a temporary surge of job demands and stress and lack of control.

Examining the impact of training efficacy on performance behaviors and project success does not reveal striking impacts and our hypotheses were not supported. However, one redeeming thought is that our training did impact important determinants of performance, namely collaborative behaviors and conflict behaviors. Chiocchio and colleagues (2012) showed that individuals' perceptions of team collaboration was predictive of individual-level performance, and also that collaboration *per se* was predictive of team performance. De Dreu & Weingart's (2003) meta-analysis showed that conflict is negatively related to performance. Hence, we conclude that although training efficacy did not impact performance directly, it did impact behaviors that are known to predict performance.

Chapter 5

Workload, Demands, Control And Perceived Stress: A Longitudinal Quantitative Examination

Introduction

In this chapter, we aim to discuss issues that interprofessional health care project team face. As studies that focus on such teams are, to our knowledge, inexistent, we will draw evidence for pertinent hypotheses to test from various streams of studies. Generally speaking, people's health is jeopardized when their job exerts high demands while limiting the ability to control what to do about it (Karasek, 1979). These types of jobs generate poor mental health, lower job satisfaction, and burnout (Baker, Israel, & Schurman, 1996; Karasek, 1979; Massé et al., 1998a, 1998b; Strazdins, D'Souza, Lim, Broom, & Rodgers, 2004; Van Der Doef, Maes, & Diekstra, 1999). Two streams of evidence are worth detailing: studies on the health care context and studies on the the context of project work.

First, for many in health care, there is an elephant in the room—that is, there are obvious problems that people choose not to talk about or tackle (Souba, Way, Lucey, Sedmak, & Notestine, 2011). In a survey on the "elephants" that plague health care, Suba et al. report that the top problems are misalignment between goals and available resources and ignoring information that clearly indicate problems with performance. These problems, combined with an inability to step back from dealing with day-to-day health care service delivery to address the organization's systemic problems with inadequate cross-functional interdependencies (Henriksen & Dayton, 2006), contribute to unhealthy workplaces. Perhaps unsurprisingly, work in the health care setting is generally considered to include very high levels of stress and a heightened workload, this particularly in recent years due to budget cutbacks of the 1990's (Vahey, Aiken, Sloane, Clarke, & Vargas, 2004).

Second, there is strong anecdotal evidence that project work is stressful (Wilemon, 2002). Recent studies show that time pressure and the number of projects taken on simultaneously, along with the time spent working on these projects predict project overload, which in turn is linked to higher stress (Nordqvist, Hovmark, & Zika-Viktorsson, 2004; Zika-Viktorsson, Sundström, & Engwall, 2006). For example, a study by Gällstedt (2003) on project team members shed light on two main sources of stress related to project work. The first concerned problems in resource allocation, namely the loss of resources or the disregard for agreements concerning obtaining important resources, a change in orientation of the project, the dependence of team members on the knowledge or expertise of one member, and the withdrawal by some members from the project team. These incidents, frequently reported by people working on projects, constitute an important source of stress by the overload of work and uncertainty they cause. The second source of stress concerned problems involving prioritization of the project, that is, the interference of other organizational tasks with project work, the repeated need to redefine the tasks and goals of the project, prioritizing other projects due to a change in policy or strategy, and finally, prematurely abandoning a project. Given the high workload and limited resources facing health care organizations, work teams in this sector seem particularly vulnerable to these stressors.

Our work comparing engineering firms (i.e., projectized organizations) to health care facilities (i.e., non-projectized organizations), suggested that project-related strain is even more acute in health care settings (Chiocchio et al., 2010). Three reasons can explain this. First, health care workers may be prone to strain and burnout (Akerboom & Maes, 2006; Peterson, Demerouti, Bergström, Asberg, & Nygren, 2008) because caring for the chronically or critically ill is physically and emotionally strenuous (Harmon, Brallier, & Brown, 2002). Second, project assignments occur over and above "regular" health care service delivery, adding to job demand.

In the next sections, we will examine evidence of relationships among workload, demands, control, stress, psychological health, organizational and social support, collaboration, conflict, various team performance determinants such as task interdependency, and finally, performance.

Project Workload, Job Demands, Job Control, and Stress

There is no universal agreement about the meaning of stress (Ganster, 2008), but it is generally accepted that occupational stress is a multifaceted construct. Stress can be seen in one of three ways (Jex, 1998). When stress is a stimulus from the work environment (e.g., increase in work load), it requires an individual to cope (e.g., compensate by working more). Viewed as a response, stress emanates from one's appreciation of job demands against personal abilities. A more complete definition combines stimulus and response into a process.

Here, stress refers to a process involving stressors, strain, and outcomes (Ganster, 2008). Strain refers "to a multitude of *negative* ways employees *may* respond when faced with stressors" (Jex, 1998, p. 2, emphasis in the original). More specifically, strain results from work situations that combine high job demands (i.e., workload, time pressure, and role conflicts), and low job control (i.e., restricted decisional latitude and power, and reduced autonomy) (D'Souza, Strazdins, Lim, Broom, & Rodgers, 2003; Van Der Doef, Maes, & Diekstra, 2000).

Job demands, such as work overload or time pressure, refer to physical, psychological, social, or organizational aspects of the job that require sustained physical, cognitive, or emotional effort (Peterson et al., 2008). Job control refers to employees' ability to make decisions about how and when they perform their work as well as the extent to which their job entails using and developing their skills (D'Souza et al., 2003).

Consequently, because of aforementioned challenges in the health care sector combined with particularities of project work, we tested the following hypotheses:

- Hy 5.1 – Project workload, job demands, and stress with be positively related.
- Hy 5.2 – Both measures of job control (i.e., decisional authority and skill discretion) will be positively related.
- Hy 5.3 – Project workload, job demands, and stress will be inversely related to job control.

Psychological Health

Psychological health is a key issue in today's high-paced society. Landy explains that "Until the mid-1980s, most jobs were solitary rather than social. That has changed. Until the mid-1980s, computers were tools used by specialists. That has changed. Until the mid-1980s, most client contact occurred between sales reps and customers. That has changed. In short, work has changed, often dramatically." (2003, p. 176–177). Perhaps unsurprisingly, susceptibility to work stress, burnout and mental health problems are increasingly challenging problems (McDaid, 2008), especially when work is poorly organized and when workplace risks have not been properly addressed (World Health Organization, 2005).

Indeed, the situation is bleak. According to the World Health Organization, the 12-month prevalence of anxiety and depression in 15 countries from Europe, the Americas, and Asia ranges between 2.4% and 18.2 % for anxiety and between 0.8% and 9.6% for depression (WHO World Mental Health Survey Consortium, 2004). Of the 15 countries studied, the higher levels of both prevalence rates are those of United States (i.e., 18.2% for anxiety and 9.6% for depression). While many assert that experiencing autonomy at work, a sense of mastery of one's environment, and positive affiliations are necessary to realize one's full potential (Ryff, 1995; Ryff & Keyes, 1995), McDaid emphasizes quite strongly that "more than two thirds of workers do not think their jobs will enhance their career prospects, nearly two thirds must work at high speed or to very tight deadlines, while more than 40% only receive low levels of assistance from line managers or are engaged in monotonous tasks. Other risk factors include a lack of control over work and lack of participation in decision making; poor social support at work and unclear management structures." (2008, p. 10).

The cost of such problems to individuals and society is high. People experiencing mental health issues are more likely to lose their job (McDaid, 2008). McDaid adds that in Europe, productivity losses due to anxiety and depression are estimated to about €100 billion. In the United States, the economic burden of depression and other mental illnesses reaches $348 a year per eligible worker (Goetzel et al., 2004). Another U.S. study shows that loss of productive time costs from depression amounts to $44 billion a year (Stewart, Ricci, Chee, Hahn, & Morganstein, 2003).

In the working population in general, perceived adverse psychosocial work environment is a risk factor for anxiety and depression (Sanne, Mykletun, Dahl, Moen, & Tell, 2005). Furthermore, anxiety and depression are usually positively associated with job demands and negatively associated with job control and support (Sanne et al., 2005). In the project context, Zika-Viktorsson et al (2006) suggest people working on projects are prone to project overload, which they define as fragmentation, disruption, and inefficiency caused by competing commitments. Others show that project-related time pressure is negatively correlated with job satisfaction (Nordqvist et al., 2004). Finally, a recent study shows a curvilinear relationship between project work load and mental health (Chiocchio et al., 2010). Initially, project work is beneficial to people's mental health. However past a certain point, as the number of projects and time spent working on projects increases, psychological distress increases and psychological well-being decreases.

This discussion leads us to the following hypotheses:

- Hy 5.4 – Project workload, job demands, and stress should be positively related to anxiety and depression.
- Hy 5.5 – Job control should be negatively related to anxiety and depression.

Support

Organizational Support

Organizational support is often defined as the support provided by managers or significant colleagues (Bliese & Castro, 2000). Vagg and Spielberger (1998) for example define organizational support as consisting of motivated coworkers doing their part and adequate supervisory support. They also include issues of participation in decisions, opportunity for advancement, recognition for good work, and good equipment.

A more focused view suggests support takes the form of organizations providing access to resources necessary for their employees to do their job (Kanter, 1986; Spreitzer, 1996). Mintzberg (1982) explains that an organization's infrastructure (i.e., methods, equipment, instruments used to produce the work—which he calls the *technical system*) influences how people perform their tasks. Rhoades and Eisenberger (2002) explain that perceived organizational support theory predicts that employees will hold negative views of their organization if they believe they are not afforded favorable working conditions and especially if the affordance of favorable working conditions is considered discretionary on the part of the organization.

The problem with project work done in an organization primarily designed to deliver service work, such as a health care facility, is that there might be a disconnect between the organization's capability to support the management of projects and the needs of and the resources afforded to employees carrying out project work. Defining supporting infrastructure as access to resources (Spreitzer, 1996), we posit that:

- Hy 5.6: Supporting infrastructure will be negatively related to project workload, job demands and stress.
- Hy 5.7: Supporting infrastructure will be positively related to job control.

Another form of support well known in the project management community is project management maturity. Project management maturity refers to an organization's sophistication and capability in managing projects (Ibbs, Reginato, & Hoon Kwak, 2007).

Some organizations' processes are well-defined, documented, and assessed regularly, while other organizations manage projects without guidance or consistency. Several conceptualizations of maturity exits. The Software Engineering Institute's maturity model has five stages (i.e., initial, repeatable, defined, managed, and optimized; Software Engineering Institute, 2005, 2006) and its success has spawned other more sophisticated maturity models suited for various industries and sectors (Gareis & Huemann, 2007). Some maturity models are more generic, such as Berkeley Project Management Process Maturity Model (i.e., ad hoc, planned, manadged at the project level, manadged at the corporate level, learning; Ibbs et al., 2007), and Kerzner's five-level model (i.e., common language, common processes, singular methodology, benchmarking and continuous improvement; 2003). Other models more specifically map organizational maturity in terms of standardization, measurement, control, and continuous improvement across multiple organizational levels such as project management, program (groups of projects), and portfolio (groups of programs) management (Project Management Institute, 2003).

Project management maturity is an important moderator in project teams because maturity is grounded in attitudes, knowledge, and actions (Andersen & Jessen, 2003) and contributes to project performance (Turner, 2009). Thus, it is not difficult to see how maturity can impact projects and people working on them. Interestingly, compared to more mature industries, multiple project assignments in less mature industries may explain lower levels of psychological well-being and higher levels of distress (Chiocchio et al., 2010).

- Hy 5.8: Maturity will be negatively related to project workload, job demands and stress.
- Hy 5.9: Maturity will be positively related to job control.

Social Support

Social Support and Performance

A ubiquitous fact associated with teams is that members must get along with each other in order to perform. Teams that work well together are more effective, more innovative and have lower levels of stress (D'Amour et al., 2005). For teams to be effective, members must become a working, cooperative entity (Rosenfeld & Richman, 1997) by showing each other social support. The underlying idea is that social support leads to better communication, and fosters a deeper, more shared commitment to team objectives and success. Results from group and team literatures in various settings seem in favor of these relationships. Indeed, social support has been used in team building exercises to improve productivity, quality of relationships, level of social skills, ability of the team to adapt to changing conditions and demands, and to increase long-term effectiveness (Rosenfeld & Richman, 1997). Moreover, social support has been related to evaluations of group cohesion and satisfaction with group experiences (Manning & Fullerton, 1988; Westre & Weiss, 1991), and satisfaction with group experiences and leadership (Garland & Barry, 1990; Schliesman, 1987; Weiss & Friedrichs, 1986). Team support has even been related to soldiers' perceptions of cohesion in their groups (Manning & Fullerton, 1988).

In interprofessional health care teams, social support would appear to be particularly relevant, as an additional source of conflict (notwithstanding the usual relationship and task conflicts that arise) is present: status and hierarchy (functional diversity in teams). Unfortunately, in health care settings, power is traditionally associated with title rather than knowledge and experience, leading to an additional strain in team dynamics, that of role conflict (Brown et al., 2010; D'Amour et al., 2005). Role boundary issues and accountability are common in health care teams, with members in less powerful positions feeling intimidated or resentful, and often silenced (Souba et al., 2011). Such a barrier in communication leads to increased conflict and increased feelings of lack of control (Brown et al., 2010).

Interestingly, individuals working in secondary health care teams reported higher levels of role clarity and social support than those working alone or in pseudo teams (i.e., teams in name alone) (Borril, West, Shapiro, & Rees, 2000). Team members described a sense of cooperation that buffered them from the negative effects of conflict. These results aren't exactly pushing for social support as a key ingredient to team success, rather a relational bonus that will help individuals cope with their conflict.

Social support, workload, demands, control, and stress

In the late 1980s, many suggested that social support was an important coping mechanism in the stressor–strain process alleviating the outcomes of strain (Van Der Doef et al., 2000). Social support is associated with lower levels of psychological stress such as anxiety, depression, and tension (Jex, 1998). Siegrist (1996) suggests that people's social roles at work provide opportunities for self-efficacy, self-esteem, and relatedness, as long as social exchanges are reciprocal and fair. His effort-reward imbalance model postulates that high effort accompanied with low reward is stressful and causes adverse health outcomes because people expect reciprocity from other actors in their social environment. Social support consists of provision of psychological and material resources from spouses, friends, family, and co-workers (S Cohen & Wills, 1985). Social support may take different forms and occur simultaneously: emotional support, informational support, social companionship, social integration (i.e., a sense of belonging to a group that shares similar interests, concerns, and recreational activities), nurturance, and instrumental support (S Cohen & Wills, 1985; Cutrona & Russell, 1987).

While research exists on the topic of social support's impact in the context of high-demand low-control jobs, results are mixed. In terms of measures and study design, studies that match specific stressors (e.g., lack of resources) with specific forms of social support (e.g., instrumental support in the form of additional resources) are not equally effective in testing complex interactions involving job demands, job control, and social support compared to main effects of social support's impact (S Cohen & Wills, 1985). For example, studies that tend to support the benefits of social support measure focused dimensions of demands and control, such as time pressure and schedule control, as opposed to broader conceptualizations such as "feelings of pressure." Finally, although much less research is focused on different forms of social support in occupational settings (Van Der Doef et al., 2000), supportive studies imply that supervisor support is more effective than co-worker support. However, this may be because supervisors are in a position to offer effective instrumental support—a more task-related form of work-related social support—while coworkers are left with providing emotional forms of social support. This makes it impossible to decipher whether it is the source or the form of social support that is effective.

Despite the challenges facing clear-cut hypotheses regarding the role of social support in general and in particular given the absence of studies on interprofessional health care project teams, this discussion nevertheless leads us to posit that high job demands and stress will drive individuals in interprofessional health care project teams to seek social support while high levels of job control will prompt team members to interact, thus fostering social support. Consequently:

- Hy 5.10: Project workload, job demands and stress will be positively associated with social support.
- Hy 5.11: Job control will not be related to social support.

Collaboration

One of the central theses of this research project and book is that social support is too narrowly defined as socio-emotional, in part because social support studies are thought of and carried out in non-professional settings. Research on providers and recipients of emotional-type social support in non-work settings suggests that social support might not be effective when providers are affected by the same stressors as recipients (Krause, 1995) as is the case in project work settings. This is because in such instances, providers may become emotionally overinvolved. The same author suggests that in an emotionally overinvolved chronically stressful context, lack of progress on the part of the recipient may cause providers to behave critically and become a stressor him/herself. Hence, emotional support might not be ideal. Instrumental support and informational support, on the other hand, are not emotional in nature and are not affected by such emotional over-involvement. Not surprisingly, in work settings requiring interprofessional collaboration, we argue that collaboration is the appropriate form of social support and an ingredient for success in teams.

Consequently, one needs to expand the concepts of informational and instrumental support to allow for more detailed and sensitive measures of supportive teamwork processes. Compared to broad or relationship-focused measures of social support, attention on the collective nature of collaboration in project work offers a more attuned perspective on the "social" part of social support at work. Furthermore, collaboration is also more instrumental and task-related, which is a more precise measure of the "support" portion of social support at work. For example, previous studies on project teams suggest that how and when team members share concerns about planning, commit to project goals (Chiocchio & Lafrenière, 2009), and solve task and coordination problems (Chiocchio, 2007), has an impact on project success.

Team processes are "members' interdependent acts that convert inputs to outcomes through cognitive, verbal, and behavioral activities directed toward organizing task-work to achieve collective goals" (Marks et al., 2001, p. 357). Processes are important from a functional perspective because they can explain how to maximize performance or outcomes as a function of various factors such as demands and control and stress. One view of collaboration is to consider it as a meta-process – as the interplay of processes such as teamwork communication, synchrony and coordination (Chiocchio, Grenier, et al., 2012).

Certain studies tend to demonstrate that different team processes are sensitive to the level of stress experienced by members. For example, teams working in medical emergencies showed that acute job demands resulting in acute emotional strain impeded teamwork in terms of coordination, communication, monitoring, and backup behavior (Gevers, Van Erven, De Jonge, Maas, & De Jong, 2010). Wegner (1986) found that acute stress negatively affected a cognitive process essential to teamwork, transactive memory, which can be construed as a cooperative division of labor for learning, remembering, and communicating relevant team knowledge. These constructs overlap with Chiocchio et al.'s (2012) view of collaboration. In a recent study of teams, Ellis (2006) found that acute stress negatively affected transactive memory of team members, impairing their ability to remember, on the one hand, who holds what information and, on the other hand, who needs what information. Roles and knowledge being markedly different from one team member to the other in interprofessional teams, transactive memory is of particular importance for group functioning.

Jex and Thomas (2003) also showed that team members who reported high levels of work-related stress had negative perceptions of collective efficacy, which represents performance expectations from the group. Groups with high collective efficacy have a strong belief in the group's ability to perform its major tasks and to overcome barriers to performance (R. A. Guzzo, Yost, Campbell, & Shea, 1993). First, the presence of stressors in work teams (role conflict, interpersonal conflict, or work-family conflict) tends to reduce the altruistic and mutual aid between team members (Jex, Adams, Bachrach, & Sorenson, 2003). Prosocial behaviors, inhibited in the presence of stress (Mathews & Canon, 1975), are essential in every team, but hold a particularly important place in the interprofessional context, where each team member possesses exclusive knowledge and skills that add a unique value to the team. By reducing these mutual aid behaviors, stress is reducing the possibility of interprofessional synergy permitted by the members' varied expertise.

This discussion on process-defined collaboration lead us to postulate that, as with social support:

- Hy 5.12: Project workload, job demands and stress will be negatively associated with collaboration.

However, whereas we posited that job control would not be related to social support, we hypotheses that:

- Hy 5.13: Job control will be positively related to collaboration.

Conflict

Williams & Allen (2008) define conflict as a team process. Others—not necessarily in opposition to the process view (see Jehn, Bezrukova, & Thatcher, 2008)—define conflict as a the team's awareness of discrepancies, incompatible wishes, or irreconcilable desires (Boulding, 1963, cited in Jehn & Mannix, 2001, p. 238) and what they do because of them (Tjosvold, 2008). There is an overwhelming body of research on conflict, the matter of which is beyond the confines of this book. Although we will provide an overview sufficient to lead to our hypotheses, we invite academics and practitioners to see De Dreu & Weingart (2003), Jehn, Bezrukova, & Thatcher (2008), and de Wit, Greer, & Jehn (in press) for reviews spanning the last decade.

Conflict Management

Since conflict is inevitable, conflict management is key. How people manage conflict depends on the situation. For example, Driskell & Salas (1991) reported that under stressful conditions, low-status members had a tendency to defer to others and were more hesitant to take action in emergencies. Subordinates were reluctant to question authority under emergency conditions, sometimes to the point of withholding valuable task information (Foushee & Helmreich, 1988). In a health care setting, the consequences of this process can be life-endangering. Also teams make trade-offs between quality and quantity of decision when under time pressure (i.e., some emphasized accuracy at the expense of making a greater number of decisions) (Adelman, Miller, Henderson, & Schoelles, 2003).

However, although situations are a factor in stress, a person's conflict style, or personal disposition, is also important (Friedman, Tidd, Currall, & Tsai, 2000). According to the dual concerns theory (Pruitt & Rubin, 1986), problem solving occurs when opposing parties both show high concern for others' objectives and views. High concern for self combined with low concern for others suggests forcing one's solution onto others. Low concern for self combined with high concern for others suggests an avoidance stance. When both parties are concerned for themselves, avoidance becomes the process by which conflict is managed. Finally moderate concern for self and others suggests making a compromise (De Dreu et al., 2001; see Appendix 6 for a graphical representation). Interestingly, how people integrate their and others' concerns determine stress (Friedman et al., 2000). Those high on concern for self have coping resources suggesting they will not be as stressed. Conversely "those who exhibit low concern for self will not be able to define the problem for the other party (or themselves), are not engaged in choosing among alternatives, and are not the ones who are taking actions. They both lack a critical resource needed to solve problems and may perceive existing problems as more threatening, thus increasing their level of stress" (Friedman et al., 2000, p. 42). Accordingly:

- Hy 5.14: People high on problem solving and high on forcing (i.e., high concern for self) will report less perceived job demands and less perceived stress.
- Hy 5.15: People high on problem solving and high on forcing (i.e., high concern for self) will report more control over their job.

Manifestations of Conflict

Jehn and her colleagues defined three types of conflict: task (i.e., disagreements about the tasks being performed), process (i.e., disagreements regarding logistical and delegation issues) and relational (i.e., disagreements and incompatibilities about issues that are personal, not work related) (Jehn, 1995; Jehn et al., 2008; Jehn & Mannix, 2001).

There is a debate about whether conflict is a positive or a negative process affecting performance (Chiocchio, Forgues, et al., 2011). Some suggest that task conflict could benefit decision-making (Jehn & Bendersky, 2003). However, as Friedman et al. say, "the problem is that task conflict usually produces relationship conflict" (2000, p. 37) and meta-analyses on conflict in teams have revealed that both relationship and task conflict have strong negative correlations with team performance and member satisfaction (De Dreu & Weingart, 2003). Not many studies are focused on process conflict. However, recent data show negative relations between process conflict and performance (Chiocchio, 2011), so it is logical to imply it impacts other variables in the same way task conflict does.

Some argue that conflict manifestations impact stress and that stress impacts conflict manifestations (Friedman et al., 2000). Furthermore, while several studies focused on the reasons given by health care professionals to explain the high levels of stress reported, few have specifically focused on interprofessional teams. This is in spite of the fact that studies showed that a major reason for high stress involves imprecise roles—particularly when the skills of different professionals overlap—which can lead to interpersonal conflict or disengagement for certain members (Arnetz, 2002). Other reasons frequently cited as contributing to stress include work overload, interpersonal conflict across professional boundaries, a too rigid or too lax respect for protocol, and tension associated to the control of knowledge and the functional boundaries of each profession (McVicar, 2003; Scholes & Vaughan, 2002). Consequently, we hypothesize that:

- Hy 5.16: Project workload, job demands, and stress will be positively related to all forms of conflict.

Ethnographic studies of conflict in organizations suggest conflicts are opportunities for high-powered people to emphasize control over others that have less power (Jehn & Bendersky, 2003). These authors, citing Pondy (1967), link bargaining conflict with expressions of autonomy. Hence, given job control encompasses decision latitude and skill discretion, there is then some logic to the following:

- Hy 5.17: Job control will be positively related to all forms of conflict.

Performance

General Determinants of Performance

Task interdependency

There are determinants of team performance that many would agree are pertinent for most teams. Task interdependency is one of them. Task interdependency is at the root of what a team is (S. G. Cohen & Bailey, 1997; Kozlowski & Ilgen, 2006). Unsurprisingly, it is also a fundamental feature of collaboration in many models in vogue in health care (see Chapter 2).

The benefits reaped from the synergy that teamwork provides rely on, among other things, the premise that the individuals composing the team are significantly interrelated (Cartwright & Zander, 1960). This interdependence, which is often the reason why the team is created (Mintzberg, 1979, 1982), emanates from the particular needs and constraints posed by the team's *raison d'être* (Goodman, 1986). Task interdependence, therefore, refers to the extent to which an individual team member needs information, materials, and support from other team members to be able to do his or her job (Van der Vegt, Van de Vliert, & Oosterhof, 2003). Although team members are dependent on each other and are required to interact and collaborate to carry out their tasks, the degree of interdependence that binds them can vary as well.

Tesluk, Mathieu, Zaccaro, and Marks (1997) have put forth a typology of interdependence. According to them, workflow requires an interdependence that is either pooled (i.e., where the independent contributions of team members are combined), sequential (i.e., requiring that a member of the team finishes his or her work before another member can begin their own tasks), reciprocal (i.e., where the work of team member A is the input of the work of member B and vice versa), or team-based (i.e., where the work is done conjunctly and simultaneously by all members without a measurable delay in the flux of work between them). These different types of workflow alter the level of interdependence between team members. For example, the tasks of a surgical team require significantly higher levels of interaction than for a manufacturing team (Gully, Incalcaterra, Joshi, & Beaubien, 2002). The importance of task interdependence in team processes has been demonstrated countless times in the scientific literature (R.A. Guzzo & Shea, 1992; Kozlowski & Bell, 2003), which is why it is considered a reliable predictor of team effectiveness. Greater task interdependence has also been linked to higher levels of team motivation (C. S. Wong & Campion, 1991), a higher sense of personal responsibility for the work of others and of the value of team rewards (Kiggundu, 1983) and of the value of team rewards (Shea & Guzzo, 1987). When interdependence is high, team members tend to communicate more, to support and influence one another regularly (Lam & Chin, 2004), as well as allocate more time to collective planning (Gundlach, Zivnuska, & Stoner, 2006). Moreover, task interdependence acts as a moderator of the relationship between cohesion and group performance (Gully, Devine, & Whitney, 1995) and of the link between team effectiveness and group performance (Gully et al., 2002).

Some studies from the health care sector have also examined the link between interdependence and team effectiveness, and have shown that interventions that sought to increase the level of interdependence between team members lead to increased levels of patient volume, length of stay and hospital charges in acute patient inpatient and trauma team settings, on top of a higher adherence by patients to treatment proposed by health care professionals (Curley, McEachern, & Speroff, 1998; Dutton et al., 2003).

Many in the health care sector would agree with Wong, DeSanctis, and Staudenmayer when they assert that "management of interdependencies constitutes a major activity of everyday work life" (2007, p. 284). These authors view managing task interdependencies as additional demands imposed on workers in terms of coordination with others, as well as more pressure to exchange resources and to manage social relations and conflict. Consequently we will test the following hypothesis.

• Hy 5.18: Project workload, job demands, and stress will be positively related to task interdependency.

Task interdependencies are related to teams' critical behavior and functions (Tesluk et al., 1997). Because tasks people perform are directly related to their skill set, what they choose to do and how they choose to do it should influence or be influenced by task interdependency. Logically then, we will test the following hypothesis:

• Hy 5.19: Job control will be positively related to task interdependence.

Goal clarity and goal similarly

Goal clarity refers to the extent to which people understand their work-related objectives and goal similarity is the extent to which individuals perceive that people on their team pursue the same goals (Sawyer, 1992; Weldon, Jehn, & Pradhan, 1991).

In a study with teachers, simple regression results showed that goal clarity was nega-tively related to job demands and perceived stress (Jacobsson, Pousette, & Thylefors, 2001). In a study with Finnish nurses, a clear goal was found to "go hand in hand with lower levels of quantitative work overload and fewer problems in occupational collaboration" (Elovainio & Kivimäki, 1996, p. 520). Furthermore, these authors also found goal clarity was posi-tively related to job control. Hence, while we did not find studies that focus on goal similar-ity, we feel poised to predict that:

- Hy 5.20: Project workload, job demands, and stress will be negatively related to goal clarity and goal similarity.
- Hy 5.21: Job control will be positively related to goal clarity and goal similarity.

Behavioral Performance

Job performance is the total expected value to the organization of behaviors individuals carries out in a given period of time (Motowidlo, 2003). While there are many types of behaviors one can enact that fall into this category, task performance is central. Task per-formance is the effectiveness with which job incumbents perform activities that contribute to the organization – and by extension – to the project team's *raison d'être* (Borman & Motowidlo, 1997). But to understand behavioral performance of people involved in project work, it is important to recognize characteristics of projects.

According to Turner and Müller (2003), three pressures result from the fact that proj-ect work involves novelty, temporariness, and progressive elaboration (Project Management Institute, 2008). These three pressures imply additional demands, increased stress, and lower job control. The first pressure, Turner and Müller explain, is that projects foster uncertainty as people cannot be sure that plans will work. Second, projects require inte-gration efforts as resources (i.e., material, but also intellectual) must be pulled together to create the project's outcome. The last pressure created by project work is urgency and need to deliver at a given point in time. Because of project uncertainty, solutions to problems rest in large part on the adequacy of information available to those in the decision-making process (Pich, Loch, & Meyer, 2002). Specifically, information is not adequate if much of it is unknown or if too much of it must be processed to assess the determine solutions' impact—which refers to ambiguity and complexity, respectively.

Project teams facing an unforeseen change "must actively incorporate the new informa-tion, develop a new model, and then replan the project in terms of a new set of activities or new policy. This evidently requires that the team be flexible" (Pich et al., 2002, p. 1014). Hence, although it has been long recognized that adaptation in the face of uncertainty is fundamental for organizational success (Katz & Kahn, 1978) and to teams (Burke, Stagl, Salas, Pierce, & Kendall, 2006; Kozlowski et al., 1999), it is particularly relevant to project teams. Specifically, it is crucial that, in addition to task proficiency, people also demonstrate adaptation and proactivity (Griffin et al., 2007). Proactivity refers to "taking initiative in improving current circumstances; it involves challenging the status quo rather than pas-sively adapting present conditions" (Crant, 2000, p. 436). Unsurprisingly, job autonomy (a component of job control) is seen as an antecedent of proactivity because it raises the controllability of tasks (Parker, Williams, & Turner, 2006).

Although few studies have investigated the effects of stress on team functioning and teamwork behaviors (Jex et al., 2003), some nonetheless shed light on the matter. For example, a study of teams working in medical emergencies showed that acute job demands resulting in acute emotional strain impeded teamwork in terms of coordination, communication, monitoring, and backup behavior (Gevers et al., 2010). Other studies show that in addition to decreasing altruistic behaviors, stress shifts team members' perspective from a broad team perspective to a more narrow, individualistic focus (Ellis, 2006) and team members exhibit reduced attention to other members and teamwork behaviors (Driskell, Salas, & Johnston, 1999). Loss of team perspective entails an impairment of two important team processes: the collective representation of the group (the mutual awareness necessary for dynamic interdependence among team members) and the collective representation of the task (how team members must interact with one another to perform the task). This change in team member perspective can lead, in turn, to diminished performance (Driskell et al., 1999).

This discussion leads us to positing the following relationships:

- Hy 5.22: Project workload, job demands, and stress will be negatively related to task proficiency, adaptive behaviors, and proactivity.
- Hy 5.23: Job control will be positively related to task proficiency, adaptive behaviors, and proactivity.

Project Performance

Project performance is what results from a team reaching project objectives. As Motowidlo emphasizes "behavior, performance, and results are not the same. Performance is the expected organizational value of what people do. Results are states or conditions of people or things that are changed by what they do in ways that contribute to or detract from organizational effectiveness. Therefore, results are the route through which an individual's behavior helps or hinders an organization in reaching its objectives, which is what makes it appealing to focus on results when considering individual performance." (2003, p. 40).

Although it makes sense to predict that individual's job control, job demands, and stress impact project performance, the prediction is distal, meaning that the link is not direct. Nevertheless, since project performance is fundamental to project management, it is pertinent to explore the extent to which team members' perceptions of project performance is affected by their level of demands, control and stress.

- Hy 5.24: Project workload, job demands, and stress will negatively impact project performance.
- Hy 5.25: Job control will positively impact project performance.

Methods
Process
Our study process and timing of our measures are detailed in Figure 1 and Table 3.1.

Measures

Project workload

We view workload as time-based demands and limitations in relation with the amount of work to perform (Beehr & Glazer, 2005). We measured project workload using Chiocchio et al.'s (2010) Project Involvement Index. This index is the result of multiplying the number of projects one is working on with the percentage of time spent on project work over a one-month period. Internal consistency indices from the original study were adequate for a two-item measure (i.e., standardized α = .69). We reach the same conclusion here with standardized α = .69 for time 1 and standardized α = .54 for time 2.

Job demands, job control, and perceived stress

Job demands refers to psychological stressors present in the work environment, such as high time pressure and workload, role conflicts, and physical and emotional demands (Karasek, 1979). Job control refers to the extent to which a person is capable of controlling their tasks and general work activity (Häusser et al., 2010). Specifically, job control refers to decisional authority (also called decisional latitude, that is, the leeway one has in deciding what to do) and skill discretion (i.e., the leeway one has in how to perform tasks). Perceived stress refers to the degree to which situations in one's life are appraised as stressful (S. Cohen et al., 1983). These measures were described in chapter 4.

Psychological health: Anxiety and depression

We measured two components of psychological health using Warr's (2005) framework, which describes psychological health-illness on various continuums. The first runs from anxiety (low pleasure-high arousal) to comfort (high pleasure-low arousal) and was measured using the Job-related anxiety-contentment scale (five items; e.g., *How many times your job made you feel worried*). The second axis ranges from depression (low pleasure-low arousal) to enthusiasm (high pleasure-high arousal) and was measured using the job-related depression-enthusiasm scale (six items; e.g., *How many times your job made you feel miserable*). Participants had to estimate the frequency with which they performed the behaviors using a five-point scale (1 = Never or almost never; 5 = Very often). After removing item 3 at both times for lack of variance, time 1 internal consistency indices in our sample were α = .81 and .71 for these dimensions respectively. At time 2, indices were α = .81 and .73.

Organizational support

Support from the infrastructure refers to the degree to which individuals perceive they have access to organizational resources they need to do their job (Kanter, 1986). We measured the infrastructure support using Spreitzer's (1996) instrument, which contains three items coming together in a single dimension (e.g., *When I need additional resources to do my job, I can usually get them*). Participants had to answer using a five-point scale (1 = Strongly disagree; 5 = Strongly agree). Internal consistency indices in our sample for this variable were α = .85.

In addition, a generic measure of organizational support, we measured support specific to projects. Project management maturity refers to an organization's sophistication and capability in managing projects (Ibbs et al., 2007). We measured project maturity with 15 of the 18 items of Kerzner's (1998) questionnaire (i.e., three items did not apply to our context).

The questionnaire measure five dimensions of maturity that are on a continuum: Embryonic (e.g., *My organization recognizes the need for project management. The need is recognized at all levels of management, including senior management*), executive (e.g., *Our executives visibly support project management through executive presentations, correspondence, and by occasionally attending project team meetings/briefings*), line management (e.g., *Our lower and middle-level line managers totally and visibly support the project management process*), growth (e.g., *My organization is committed to quality up-front planning. We try to do the best we can at planning*), and maturity (e.g., *Our organization has successfully integrated cost and schedule control together for both managing projects and reporting status*). Participants had to answer using a five-point scale (1 = Strongly disagree; 5 = Strongly agree). Once items 10 and 15 were removed for lack of variance, internal consistency indices in our sample were α = .73, .72, .74, .60, and .72 for these dimensions, respectively.

Social support

Social provision refers to relationships, perceptions, and transactions that help individuals master emotional distress, share tasks, receive advice, learn skills, and obtain material assistance (Pierce, Sarason, Sarason, Joseph, & Henderson, 1996). We measured social provision with Cutrona & Russell's (1987) 24-item questionnaire. The questionnaire measure six dimensions of social provision: Guidance refers to provision of advice or information (e.g., *There is someone I could talk to about important decisions in my life*); reliable alliance is the assurance that others can be counted upon for tangible assistance (e.g., *There are people I can depend on to help me if I really need it*); reassurance of worth is the recognition of one's competence, skills, and value by others (e.g., *I have relationships where my competence and skill are recognized*); opportunity for nurturance is the sense that others rely upon one for their well-being (e.g., *I feel personally responsible for the well-being of another person*); attachment refers to the emotional closeness from which one derives a sense of security (e.g., *I feel a strong emotional bond with at least one other person*), and finally, social integration is a sense of belonging to a group that shares similar interests, concerns, and recreational activities (e.g., *There are people who enjoy the same social activities I do*). Participants had to answer using a five-point scale (1 = Strongly disagree; 5 = Strongly agree). Item 22 had to be removed at both times because of a lack of variance. At time 1, internal consistency indices in our sample were α = 70, .70, .69, .75, .67, and .45 for these dimensions, respectively. At time 2, indices were α = 70, .54, .73, .49, .67, and .48.

Collaboration

Collaborative work refers to teamwork communication, synchrony, explicit coordination, implicit coordination (Chiocchio, Grenier, et al., 2012), and interprofessional processes (Vinokur-Kaplan, 1995). These measures were described in chapter 4.

Conflict handling style

Le Dutch test for Conflict Handling (De Dreu et al., 2001) was used to evaluate individuals' personal style of conflict management, which refers to strategies used in response to the experience of conflict (Van de Vliert, 1997). This measure is based on dual concerns theory (Pruitt & Rubin, 1986) and includes 20 items divided into five sub-dimensions: yielding (e.g., *I give in to the wishes of the other party*), forcing (e.g., *I fight for a good outcome for myself*), compromising (e.g., *I insist we both give in a little*), avoiding (e.g., *I avoid a confrontation about our differences*), and problem-solving (e.g., *I examine issues until I find a solution that really satisfies me and the other party*). Participants had to estimate the frequency with which they performed the behaviors using a five-point scale (1 = Never or almost never; 5 = Very often). Internal consistency indices in our sample were α = 73, .70, .86, .86, and .80 for these dimensions, respectively.

Conflict

Conflict is an awareness on the part of the parties involved of discrepancies, incompatible wishes, or irreconcilable desires and what people do because of them (Chiocchio, Forgues, et al., 2011). We measured conflicts with Jehn & Mannix's (2001) nine-item questionnaire, as we described fully in chapter 4.

Task Interdependency

Task interdependency refers to the extent to which group members interact and depend on one another to accomplish the work (Campion et al., 1993). We measured task interdependency with Campion et al.'s three-item questionnaire (e.g., *Other members of my project team depend on me to accomplish their tasks*). Participants had to answer using a five-point scale (1 = Strongly disagree; 5 = Strongly agree). Internal consistency indices in our sample for this variable were α = .68 for both times 1 and 2; however, item 3 had to be removed at time 2 because of lack of variance.

Goal clarity and similarity

Goal clarity refers to the extent to which the outcome goals and objectives of the job are clearly stated and well defined (Sawyer, 1992). We measured goal clarity with Sawyer's five-item questionnaire (e.g., *The expected results of my work are clear*). Participants had to answer using a five-point scale (1 = Strongly disagree; 5 = Strongly agree). Internal consistency indices in our sample for this variable were α = .94 at time 1 and .92 at time 2.

Goal similarity refers to the extent to which team members perceive that they share the same goals regarding the project (Weldon et al., 1991). We measured goal similarity with (Jehn, 1995) three-item questionnaire (e.g., *The main goals of my project team are the same for all members*). Participants had to answer using a five-point scale (1 = Strongly disagree; 5 = Strongly agree). Internal consistency indices in our sample for this variable were α = .83 for both times 1 and 2.

Behavioral performance

Performance is a multilevel construct: individual, team, and project. Individual performance refers to individuals' behaviors contributing to individual effectiveness, while team member performance refers to individuals' behaviors contributing to team effectiveness (Griffin et al., 2007; Motowidlo, 2003). More details can be found in chapter 4.

Project performance

Two elements were assessed. First, regular assessment of a project refers to the monitoring of defined activities to ensure that the project objectives are achieved (Stratman & Roth, 2002). Second, we also measured project performance as to the extent to which a project is completed in time, within budget and demonstrates a quality that satisfies client/customer requirements (Kerzner, 2003). More information on these measures can be found in chapter 4.

Results

Descriptive Results

Tables 5.1 and 5.2 show descriptive statistics pertaining to stress, strain, demands, and control measures. Before we examine specific hypotheses, a look at some socio-demographic is in order (Table 5.1).

Interestingly, Table 5.1 tends to show that perceived demands and age and experience, but not tenure, are positively related. All other variables, including demands at time 2, are unrelated. It is possible that those with more experience (and therefore older individuals) perceive more demands because more demands are placed on them at the beginning of the project.

Table 5.1: Means, Standard Deviation, and Intercorrelations for Scores on Measures on Project Workload, Demands, and Control with Age, Years of Experience and Tenure, Preference for Group Work, and Informational Role Self-Efficacy

	Age	Years of Experience	Tenure
T1 Project Involvement Index	.06	-.13	-.21
T1 Demands	.35***	.25**	-.01
T1 Control Decision Authority	.15	-.02	.13
T1 Control Skill Discretion	.19	.08	.11
T1 Perceived Stress	.01	.09	-.03
T2 Project Involvement Index	-.06	-.14	.02
T2 Demands	.09	.05	.03
T2 Control Decision Authority	.14	-.03	.04
T2 Control Skill Discretion	.20	.17	.08
T2 Perceived Stress	-.07	-.05	.05
M	43.57	16.53	5.75
StDev	11.04	10.73	7.62

Note: M = mean; StDev = Standard deviation.
$* p < .1$; $** p < .05$; $*** p < .01$.
N = 53 to 59

Table 5.2: Means, Standard Deviation, and Intercorrelations for Scores on Measures on Project Workload, Demands, Control, and Stress

	A	B	C	D	E	F	G	H	I	J
A. T1 Project Involvement Index	–	.25*	.20	.29**	-.03	.61***	.49***	.21	.27*	.06
B. T1 Demands		–	-.11	.24*	.35***	.17	.50***	-.12	.01	.17
C. T1 Control Decision Authority			–	.41***	-.44***	.26*	.04	.64***	.31**	-.48***
D. T1 Control Skill Discretion				–	-.05	.18	.40***	.40***	.70***	-.04
E. T1 Perceived Stress					–	.13	.20	-.25*	-.09	.61***
F. T2 Project Involvement Index						–	.30**	.31**	.23*	.14
G. T2 Demands							–	.15	.45***	.15
H. T2 Control Decision Authority								–	.53***	-.42***
I. T2 Control Skill Discretion									–	-.18
J. T2 Perceived Stress										–
M	21.77	3.01	3.65	4.18	2.24	21.27	2.88	3.57	4.12	2.28
StDev	25.16	1.12	0.70	0.55	0.50	36.09	0.97	0.73	0.60	0.58

Note: M = mean; $StDev$ = Standard deviation.
* $p < .1$; ** $p < .05$; *** $p < .01$.
N = 51 to 61

Let us now turn to Table 5.2, which shows mean frequency level of how people perceive demands, control, and incidents causing them stress.

Project workload is at about 21 but varies more at time 2 and earlier in the project. The Project Involvement Index is made up of the product of number of projects and percentage of time spent working on projects in the last month. At time 1, mean number of projects was 4.39 ($SD = 3.32$) and mean percentage spent on projects was 38% ($SD = 30\%$). At time 2, mean number of projects was 4.28 ($SD = 4.70$) and mean percentage spent on projects was 37% ($SD = 30\%$). Compared to past studies (Chiocchio et al., 2010), professionals were involved in about twice as many projects. However, they were not given more time to work on these projects.

Overall means in Table 5.2 vary from *occasionally* for stress to between *relatively often* to *very often* for job demands and job control. Hypotheses 5.1 to 5.3 stated demands and stress would be positively correlated to each other, decision authority and skill discretion would be positively correlated to each other, and that these two sets would be inversely related to each other. Job demands and stress are positively correlated, so are both forms of job control. Although statistically significant correlations between stress and decision authority are negative (i.e., they vary between $r = -.42$ and $-.48$), those with job demands tend to be positively related (e.g., $r = .24$ and .45 at time 1 and 2, respectively). Project workload is positively related to job demands and job control with correlations varying between $r = .23$ and $.49$). Hence, there is moderate support for Hy 5.1, strong support for Hy 5.2, but mixed results for Hy 5.3.

Comparing Time 1 and Time 2 measures does not reveal variations, meaning that levels appear constant throughout the project life (see Figure 1 for average time between measurements). Correlations for each of these constructs over time are high and vary between $r = .50$ and $.70$. Together with similar means over time, this implies that early perceived intensity is a good predictor of later intensity. Furthermore, demands and stress at time one are correlated while at time 2 they are not.

Psychological health: Anxiety and Depression

Table 5.3 shows the relationships between workload and psychological health variables over time.

Results in Table 5.3 show that mean levels of perceived anxiety and depression oscillate around 2, meaning that people reported feeling tense (anxiety) or miserable (depression)

Table 5.3: Means, Standard Deviation, and Intercorrelations for Scores on Measures on Project Workload, Demands, Control, and Stress on Anxiety and Depression

	1	2	3	4
T1 Project Involvement Index	.03	-.27**	.20	.00
T1 Demands	.36***	-.04	.31**	.32**
T1 Control Decision Authority	-.44***	-.43***	-.26*	-.35**
T1 Control Skill Discretion	0.11	-.58***	.00	-.40**
T1 Perceived Stress	.59***	.37***	.58***	0.26*
T2 Project Involvement Index			.26*	-.06
T2 Demands			.40***	-0.12
T2 Control Decision Authority			-.32**	-.44***
T2 Control Skill Discretion			-.08	-.57***
T2 Perceived Stress			.74***	.54***
M	2.76	1.88	2.79	1.80
StDev	0.66	0.54	0.72	0.51

Note: M = mean; StDev = Standard deviation.
1 = T1 Anxiety, 2 = T1 Depression, 3 = T2 Anxiety, 4 = T2 Depression.
$* p < .1; ** p < .05; *** p < .01$.
N = 50 to 61

once in a while in the last month. Feelings of anxiety seem to occur more often than feelings of depression, and these levels stay stable throughout the projects' life-cycle. As predicted by Hy 5.4, demands and stress are positively related to anxiety and depression. In Hy 5.5 we predicted that skill discretion and decision authority are forms of control that are negatively related to anxiety and depression. We found moderate to strong support this hypothesis.

Support

Organizational support

Table 5.4 shows how measures of organizational support prior to the projects' onset relate to impressions of demands, control, and stress later in the project life.

Organizational support instruments measured the extent to which the team members' perceived their organization capable to help them work and manage their projects. Mean levels are not particularly high, but interestingly, as we move from a general perspective

Table 5.4: Means, Standard Deviation, and Intercorrelations for Scores of Measures of Project Workload, Demands, Control, and Stress on Organizational Support

	1	2	3	4	5	6
T1 Project Involvement Index	-.17	-.08	-.26**	.21	-.26**	-.20
T1 Demands	-.08	.13	-.17	.11	-.13	.05
T1 Control Decision Authority	-.01	.21	.17	.01	.05	-.09
T1 Control Skill Discretion	-.02	.01	-.06	-.05	-.17	-.07
T1 Perceived Stress	.13	-.09	-.10	.05	-.21	-.17
T2 Project Involvement Index	-.14	-.10	-.04	-.31**	-.27*	-.29**
T2 Demands	-.01	-.08	-.27*	-.12	-.40***	-.19
T2 Control Decision Authority	.18	.14	.15	-.13	-.06	-.16
T2 Control Skill Discretion	-.01	-.03	.04	-.07	-.17	-.15
T2 Perceived Stress	.03	-.13	-.14	-.14	-.07	.07
M	3.37	3.32	3.22	3.26	2.99	2.69
StDev	0.79	0.71	0.78	0.86	0.62	0.75

Note: *M* = mean; *StDev* = Standard deviation.
1 = Supporting infrastructure, 2 = Embryonic maturity, 3 = Executive maturity, 4 = Line management maturity, 5 = Growth maturity, 6 = Maturity.
$* p < .1$; $** p < .05$; $*** p < .01$.
N = 53 to 59

(i.e., support from the infrastructure) to Kerzner's (2003) five levels of maturity, one can see a downward trend. Specifically, people's level of agreement goes from between neutrality and agreement at one end to between neutrality and disagreement at the other. This tends to confirm Kerzner's model stating that project maturity progresses from basic support toward more elaborated forms of support, but that most organizations are at the lower end of the continuum. We posited in Hy 5.6 to 5.9 that job demands and stress will be negatively related to organizational support and that job control will be positively related to organizational support. Except for project workload, correlation trends are not apparent, despite a few negative correlations with demands at time 2. We conclude that overall, there is no support or moderate support for our hypotheses.

Social support

Table 5.5 displays relationships between workload perceptions and type of social support.

First, we can see that the form of social support for which people seem to agree using more at both times is reliable alliance (i.e., the assurance that others can be counted upon for tangible assistance). Second, opportunity of nurturance (i.e., the sense that people rely

Table 5.5: Means, Standard Deviation, and Intercorrelations for Scores of Measures of Project Workload, Demands, Control, and Stress on Social Support

	1	2	3	4	5	6	7	8	9	10	11	12
T1 Project Involvement Index	.17	.01	.16	-.26**	.00	.02	-.02	.24*	.21	-.12	-.09	-.04
T1 Demands	.30**	.17	.22*	.04	.05	.33***	.18	.11	.22	.07	.05	.07
T1 Control Decision Authority	.11	.18	-.02	.16	.15	.02	.10	.33**	.11	.12	.18	.15
T1 Control Skill Discretion	.34***	.13	.25**	.09	.30**	.24*	.19	.31**	.40***	.14	.17	.14
T1 Perceived Stress	.01	-.14	.23*	-.20	-.17	.08	-.07	.06	.21	-.18	-.08	-.08
T2 Project Involvement Index							.11	.31**	.17	.12	.01	.04
T2 Demands							.10	.15	.27**	.07	.12	-.03
T2 Control Decision Authority							.00	.35***	.20	.16	.09	.01
T2 Control Skill Discretion							.17	.39***	.34**	.22	.17	.09
T2 Perceived Stress							-.11	-.14	.01	-.14	-.07	-.14
M	4.28	3.63	3.57	4.14	4.43	4.19	4.22	3.80	3.47	4.19	4.33	4.15
StDev	0.50	0.59	0.76	0.51	0.49	0.56	0.52	0.45	0.62	0.52	0.47	0.56

Note: M = mean; StDev = Standard deviation.
1 = T1 Attachment, 2 = T1 Social integration, 3 = T1 Opportunity for nurturance, 4 = T1 Reassurance of worth, 5 = T1 Reliable alliance, 6 = T1 Guidance,
7 = T2 Attachment, 8 = T2 Social integration, 9 = T2 Opportunity for nurturance, 10 = T2 Reassurance of worth, 11 = T2 Reliable alliance, 12 = T2 Guidance.
* $p < .1$; ** $p < .05$; *** $p < .01$.
N = 51 to 60

on each other for their well-being) is the form of social support people agree that they are using less. Accordingly, it seems that people agree or fully agree that reliable alliances are an important form of social support throughout the projects' lives, whereas they are neutral or in agreement regarding opportunity for nurturance. Of all variables, perceived stress is the least related to any forms of social support. Demands at times 1 and 2 correlate positively with attachment, opportunity for nurturance, and guidance. Both forms of control correlate with a number of forms of social support. However, skill discretion is the strongest predictor of most forms of social support within and between times. Specifically as perceptions of skill discretion at time 1 increases, so does their use of attachment, opportunity for nurturance, reliable alliances, and guidance at time 1 and social integration and opportunity for nurturance at time 2. People's skill discretion in later phases of the project increases with preferences for social integration and opportunity for nurturance at time 2. Overall, these results tend to confirm hypotheses 5.10 and 5.11.

Collaboration

As discussed earlier, collaboration is a more task-related version of support at work. Table 5.6 displays results that pertain to collaboration.

Table 5.6: Means, Standard Deviation, and Intercorrelations for Scores on Measures of Project Workload, Demands, Control, and Stress on Collaboration

	1	2	3	4	5	6	7	8	9	10
T1 Project Involvement Index	.19	.03	.18	.04	-.01	.00	-.12	-.04	-.06	-.11
T1 Demands	-.18	-.27**	-.08	.01	.07	-.12	-.10	-.04	-.01	.17
T1 Control Decision Authority	.15	.10	.16	.12	.20	.08	.04	.04	-.06	.18
T1 Control Skill Discretion	.24*	.17	.31**	.32**	.22*	.04	.00	.11	.01	.27*
T1 Perceived Stress	-.24*	-.23*	-.11	-.07	-.30**	-.05	-.03	-.01	.04	-.19
T2 Project Involvement Index						.10	-.06	.07	.11	.00
T2 Demands						.02	.05	.08	.02	.00
T2 Control Decision Authority						.33**	.19	.18	.18	.12
T2 Control Skill Discretion						.22	.16	.16	.21	.21
T2 Perceived Stress						-.22	-.25*	-.15	-.13	-.35***
M	3.59	3.49	3.33	2.93	3.72	3.70	3.57	3.48	3.26	3.76
StDev	0.96	1.03	1.12	0.98	0.46	0.93	1.04	1.06	0.93	0.42

Note: M = mean; StDev = Standard deviation.
1 = T1 Teamwork communication, 2 = T1 Synchronicity, 3 = T1 Explicit Coordination, 4 = T1 Implicit Coordination, 5 = T1 Interprofessional, 6 = T2 Teamwork communication, 7 = T2 Synchronicity, 8 = T2 Explicit Coordination, 9 = T2 Implicit Coordination, 10 = T2 Interprofessional.
* $p < .1$; ** $p < .05$; *** $p < .01$.
N = 50 to 60

With mean levels of collaborative processes (i.e., dimensions 1 to 4 and 6 to 9 in Table 5.5 of Chiocchio, Grenier, et al., 2012's instrument) between 3 and 4, team members engage "relatively often" to "often" in interactive behaviors. Regarding the extent to which people agree with manifestations interprofessional collaboration behaviors (dimensions 5 and 10 in Table 5.5 Vinokur-Kaplan, 1995's instrument), mean levels vary between neutrality and agreement. Although there are no differences between times, all levels increase somewhat over the weeks between time 1 and time 2.

Except for increasing levels of demands' relationship with decreasing levels of synchrony at time 1 ($r = -.27$), demands do not seem to be related to collaboration. However, stress at times 1 and 2 seem to be negatively related to many components of collaboration. Specifically, as perception of stress increases at time 1, people report initiating less teamwork communication ($r = -.24$), being less synchronized ($r = -.23$), and report being less inclined to collaborate across professional boundaries ($r = -.30$) at time 1. Whereas stress at time 1 does not seem to co-vary with collaboration components at time 2, stress and collaboration components at time 2 show similar negative trends as correlations within time 1. As posited with Hy 5.12, our results show that job demands and stress are negatively related to some accounts of collaborative behaviors, but not all.

Decision authority at time 1 is not a variable that seem to exert an effect on collaboration. However at time 2, decision authority correlates positively with teamwork communication ($r = .33$), suggesting that as impressions of the latitude with which one performs his or her tasks increases, so does perceptions of how the team members exchange information, share knowledge, understand each other, and share resources. Skill discretion seems to exert the most influence on reporting of collaborative behaviors at time 1 and most notably at interprofesional collaboration behaviors weeks later at time 2 ($r = 27$). Hence, our contention that job control may facilitate collaborative behaviors (i.e., Hy 5.13) seems confirmed, but not in an overwhelming manner.

Conflict

Conflict handling

In our study, we measured two sets of variables regarding conflict. Table 5.7 shows results that pertain with people's preferred style of handling conflicts, and Table 5.8 examines frequencies of conflict behaviors.

Because they represent a somewhat stable personality disposition, measures of conflict handling were taken at time 0; that is, prior to the projects' initiation.

Results show that everybody uses each style at least occasionally. Specifically, mean levels show that the least frequently used style is forcing (i.e., occasionally), and the two styles people most frequently resort to is making a compromise and problem-solving (i.e., between relatively often and often). The extent to which these styles impact later perceptions of demands, control, and stress is shown in terms of correlations. Interestingly, as preference for manifesting behaviors consistent with making compromises increases, subsequent perceptions of demands at time 1 increases as well ($r = .38$). An inverse trend is apparent between tendency to engage in making compromises and perceived stress at time 1 and, most notably, at time 2 ($r = -.30$). Preference for engaging in problem-solving

Table 5.7: Means, Standard Deviation, and Intercorrelations for Scores of Project Workload, Demands, Control, and Stress on Conflict-Handling Style

	1	2	3	4	5
T1 Project Involvement Index	-.11	.01	.10	.18	.07
T1 Demands	-.11	.14	.38***	.18	.01
T1 Control Decision Authority	-.02	-.11	.18	.27**	.29**
T1 Control Skill Discretion	.00	.22*	.24*	.29**	.03
T1 Perceived Stress	.01	-.02	-.24	-.19	-.13
T2 Project Involvement Index	-.21	-.13	.10	.15	.21
T2 Demands	-.27**	.10	.15	.05	.02
T2 Control Decision Authority	-.03	-.20	.11	.30**	.19
T2 Control Skill Discretion	.07	.11	.20	.07	-.09
T2 Perceived Stress	-.17	-.06	-.30**	-.39***	-.23
M	2.97	2.61	3.68	3.75	2.09
StDev	1.05	0.58	0.77	0.71	0.56

Note: *M* = mean; *StDev* = Standard deviation.
1 = TO Avoiding, 2 = TO Yielding, 3 = TO Making a compromise, 4 = TO Problem-Solving, 5 = TO Forcing.
* $p < .1$; ** $p < .05$; *** $p < .01$.
N = 53 to 59

behaviors does not co-vary with demands. However, this style tends to be positively associated with control at times 1 and 2, while as preference for problem-solving increases, stress seem to diminish, more notably later in the project (i.e., $r = -.30$ and $-.39$). Earlier, we had posited that scores on styles indicative of high concern for self (i.e., problem solving and forcing) would be positively related to job demands, job control, and stress (i.e., Hy V.14 and V.15). Results are mixed.

Manifestations of conflict

Turning now to manifestation of conflict and Table 5.8, mean frequency levels show that conflict behaviors are, at most, only occasionally enacted.

It is interesting to note that project workload at time 1 is positively related to task conflict at times 1 and 2. Also, job demands at time 1 and 2 impact task and process conflict at time 2. Hence, as people perceive demands as increasing, later manifestations of task and process conflict also increase. The same trend is observable for stress. Both variables denoting control over one's job impact task and process conflict. Whereas increased levels of decision authority and skill discretion seem to reduce task

Table 5.8: Means, Standard Deviation, and Intercorrelations for Scores of Project Workload, Demands, Control, and Stress on Conflicts

	1	2	3	4	5	6
T1 Project Involvement Index	.02	.22*	.01	-.04	.24*	.16
T1 Demands	.03	.08	.14	.01	.29**	.33**
T1 Control Decision Authority	-.11	.01	-.23*	.19	.01	.09
T1 Control Skill Discretion	-.13	-.04	-.22*	.15	.14	.34**
T1 Perceived Stress	.04	.07	.24*	.04	.38***	.17
T2 Project Involvement Index				-.05	.13	.02
T2 Demands				.18	.33**	.42***
T2 Control Decision Authority				.26*	.05	.18
T2 Control Skill Discretion				.25*	.09	.29**
T2 Perceived Stress				.09	.40***	.25*
M	1.40	1.68	1.48	1.32	1.62	1.44
StDev	0.43	0.55	0.53	0.40	0.54	0.48

Note: M = mean; $StDev$ = Standard deviation.
PII = Project Involvement Index; DA = Decision Authority; SD = Skill Discretion.
1 = T1 Relational Conflict, 2 = T1 Task Conflict, 3 = T1 Process Conflict, 4 = T2 Relational Conflict,
5 = T2 Task Conflict, 6 = T2 Process Conflict.
* $p < .1$; ** $p < .05$; *** $p < .01$.
N = 51 to 60

and process conflict at time 1, the trend is reversed at time 2. Specifically, as perceptions of skill discretion early in the project increase, so do manifestations of process conflict. And as perceptions of decision authority and skill discretion increase, so does self-reported manifestations of relational and, for skill discretion, process conflict. Our hypotheses suggested that job demands, job control, and stress would all be positively related to every form of conflict (i.e., Hy 5.16 and 5.17). For the most part this contention is moderately confirmed except for measures of job control within time 1 where the trend is negative.

Performance

General determinants of performance

Before we move on to actual performance, it is worthwhile to examine (see Table 5.9) the extent to which general determinants of performance interact with demands, control and stress.

Table 5.9: Means, Standard Deviation, and Intercorrelations for Scores of Project Workload, Demands, Control, and Stress on Determinants of Team Performance

	1	2	3	4	5	6
T1 Project Involvement Index	.11	.02	-.10	.21	-.10	-.24*
T1 Demands	.11	.09	.05	.05	.06	-.03
T1 Control Decision Authority	.02	.25*	.20	.20	.34**	.37***
T1 Control Skill Discretion	.31**	.09	.21	.31**	.29**	.19
T1 Perceived Stress	.01	-.19	-.25*	-.20	-.24*	-.30**
T2 Project Involvement Index				.28**	.09	.07
T2 Demands				.26*	.11	-.06
T2 Control Decision Authority				.24*	.33**	.34**
T2 Control Skill Discretion				.32**	.43***	.29**
T2 Perceived Stress				-.21	-.37***	-.27*
M	3.84	3.97	4.01	3.74	4.23	4.04
StDev	0.79	0.51	0.56	0.79	0.51	0.52

Note: M = mean; $StDev$ = Standard deviation.
1 = T1 Task interdependency, 2 = T1 Goal clarity, 3 = T1 Goal similarity, 4 = T2 Task interdependency, 5 = T1 Goal clarity, 6 = T2 Goal similarity.
* $p < .1$; ** $p < .05$; *** $p < .01$.
N = 51 to 60

Levels of most measures in this study do not vary between times 1 and 2. In the case of measures depicted in Table 5.9, however, goal clarity seem did increase somewhat ($t = -2.95$, $p < .005$), yet not in a truly relevant way (i.e., from 4.01 at time 1 to 4.23 at time 2). Nevertheless, project workload, impressions of demands, control, and stress co-vary in meaningful ways with general determinants, especially those at time 2. Most notably, increases in stress at time 1 seem to induce reduced goal clarity and goal similarity (i.e., $r = -.24$ and $-.30$, respectively, at time 2). In addition, decision authority at time 1 increases as perceptions of goal clarity and goal similarity increase later in the project (i.e., $r = .34$ and .37 respectively at time 2). The same is true for the skill discretion regarding task interdependency and goal clarity (i.e., $r = .31$ and .29, respectively, at time 2). Measures within time 2 show similar and larger trends.

First, we had posited that managing task interdependency was an additional demand requiring management (i.e., Hy 5.18). Time 1 measures did not correlate with task interdependence at time 1 or later at time 2. However, within time 2, demands and task interdependency are related. We also posited that job control would facilitate task interdependency (i.e., Hy 5.19). This hypothesis is supported as both measures of job control, but especially skill discretion, are positively related to task interdependency.

Regarding goal clarity and goal similarity, we suggested that project workload, demands, and stress would correlate negatively (i.e., Hy 5.20) and that control would see positive correlations with these constructs (i.e., Hy 5.21). We find weak to moderate support for these hypotheses.

Behavioral performance

The next two tables examine the relationships between demands, control, and stress with behaviors people enact with regard to proficiency, adaptability, and proactivity. Table 5.10 show results pertaining to performance behaviors people do, on the one hand, to perform their tasks better, adapt, or be proactive (i.e., dimensions 1, 2, 3, 7, 8, and 9 in the table) and on the other hand, what they do to make their team better able to do its tasks, adapt, and be proactive (i.e., dimensions 4, 5, 6, 10, 11, and 12 in the table).

Mean levels of these measures show that people report enacting performance behaviors between *relatively often* to *often*. As suggested in Hy 5.22 project workload is positively

Table 5.10: Means, Standard Deviation, and Intercorrelations for Scores of Project Workload, Demands, Control, and Stress on Behavioral Performance

	1	2	3	4	5	6	7	8	9	10	11	12
T1 Project Involvement Index	.23*	.21	.21	.17	.27**	.33***	.07	-.02	-.02	-.01	-.06	.00
T1 Demands	-.03	.08	.09	.02	.10	.29**	.01	-.06	.00	-.05	-.09	-.01
T1 Control Decision Authority	.38***	.25**	.26**	.27**	.29**	.27**	.28**	.23*	.14	.31**	.33**	.38**
T1 Control Skill Discretion	.36***	.38***	.35***	.34***	.47***	.40***	.20	.25*	.28*	.23	.23	.25*
T1 Perceived Stress	-.24*	-.07	-.10	-.23*	-.17	-.14	-.09	-.12	-.07	-.13	-.12	-.20
T2 Project Involvement Index							.09	.08	.09	.06	.03	.11
T2 Demands							.15	.19	.11	.18	.05	.21
T2 Control Decision Authority							.37***	.32**	.23*	.41***	.37***	.38***
T2 Control Skill Discretion							.34**	.32**	.28**	.37***	.34**	.29**
T2 Perceived Stress							-.22	-.16	-.07	-.20	-.24*	-.26*
M	3.98	3.84	3.55	3.90	3.72	3.37	4.01	3.80	3.64	4.02	3.73	3.32
StDev	0.97	0.96	1.01	0.87	0.94	1.05	0.98	0.97	1.06	0.90	1.02	1.09

Note: *M* = mean; *StDev* = Standard deviation.
  1 = T1 individual task proficiency, 2 = T1 individual adaptability, 3 = T1 individual proactivity, 4 = T1 team proficiency, 5 = T1 team adaptability
  6 = T1 team proactivity, 7 = T2 individual task proficiency, 8 = T2 individual adaptability, 9 = T2 individual proactivity, 10 = T2 team proficiency,
  11 = T2 team adaptability, 12 = T2 team proactivity.
  * $p < .1$; ** $p < .05$; *** $p < .01$.
  N = 51 to 60

related to many measures of behavioral performance, but only at time 1. Contrary to what we posited in Hy 5.22, job demands do not seem to impact these behaviors except for a positive effect on team proactivity ($r = .29$). In line with our contention in Hy 5.22 for stress, stress seems to co-vary negatively with task proficiency ($r = -0.24$) and team adaptation and proactivity ($r = -.24$ and $-.26$, respectively). As predicted in Hy 5.23, as feelings of decisional authority and skill discretion increase, so do self-reported levels of almost all performance behaviors.

Project performance

Participants in our study not only reported on their behavioral performance, they also reported on the extent to which they assessed the progression of their project and the extent to which they felt they met time, budget, and functional requirements. Table 5.11 shows people's ratings to be between *neutrality* and *agreement*.

Table 5.11: Means, Standard Deviation, and Intercorrelations for Scores on Measures of Project Workload, Demands, Control, and Stress on Project Performance and Regular Assessments of Project

	1	2	3	4	5	6
T1 Project Involvement Index	.09	-.09	.09	.02	-.13	-.29**
T1 Demands	-.08	-.26**	-.12	.16	.01	-.08
T1 Control Decision Authority	.18	-.03	.05	.02	.07	-.08
T1 Control Skill Discretion	.32**	.08	.26**	.18	-.13	-.01
T1 Perceived Stress	-.11	-.19	-.15	.16	.11	.03
T2 Project Involvement Index				.17	.06	-.05
T2 Demands				.12	.03	.04
T2 Control Decision Authority				.13	.18	.01
T2 Control Skill Discretion				.17	.07	.04
T2 Perceived Stress				-.07	-.32**	-.09
M	3.61	3.24	3.43	3.78	3.25	3.63
StDev	0.78	0.55	0.67	0.71	0.65	0.71

Note: M = mean; $StDev$ = Standard deviation.
1 = T1 regular assessment of project performance, 2 = T1 Time and Budget performance,
3 = T1 Functional performance, 4 = T2 regular assessment of project performance, 5 = T2 Time and Budget performance, 6 = T2 Functional performance.
* $p < .1$; ** $p < .05$; *** $p < .01$.
N = 51 to 60

Overall, individuals' perceptions of project workload, demands, control, and stress seem to not relate strongly or consistently with their reports of project performance. The few statistically significant correlations do show the same trends: negative in terms of workload, demands, and stress, and positive in terms of control. Hence, when correlations are statistically significant, they offer support for Hypotheses 5.24 and 5.25.

Results Summary and Preliminary Discussion

This chapter aimed to understand the extent of the impact of workload, job demands, job control, and stress on members of interprofessional health care project teams. Table 5.12 shows a summary of our results.

Levels and Consistency of Project Workload, Job Demands, Job Control, Stress, and Psychological Health

An examination of items comprising measured dimensions (see Appendix 3) provides an interesting analysis of the results. Regarding job demands, in the beginning of the project, people reported the need to work fast and intensely relatively often. They also reported having to address the needs of different groups relatively often as well. Weeks later, once teams were well into the execution of their project, these levels decreased somewhat to occasional occurrences. Perceived stress remained stable across both times team members were assessed, with some occasionally reporting being upset with unforeseen events, having difficulty coping, or being angered with things outside of their control. Levels of job control were higher than job demands and stress at both times. In terms of decision authority, team members often expressed being able to choose what to do at work, having a say in their pace of work, and how they could plan their work. Skill discretion was higher. Specifically, team members indicated that they very often had the opportunity to learn new things, take the initiative, and use their skills and expertise. Overall, it appears that project team members felt high levels of control regarding moderate levels of demands. Generally speaking, stress and job demands are positively related, while stress and decision authority are inversely related.

Team members occasionally felt tension and anxiety while reporting even lower frequencies of feelings of gloom and depression. While infrequent, these feelings were positively related to job demands and stress and negatively related with decision authority and skill discretion. Moreover, job demands and stress at time 1 had a lasting impact on thoughts of anxiety and depression weeks later at time 2.

Support

The extent to which organizations support their employees' capacity to perform their job should reduce job demands and stress and foster job control. However, when it comes to a supporting infrastructure, team members neither agreed nor disagreed that they had access to resources needed to do their job or to support new ideas. Moreover, this form of organizational support was unrelated to job demands, job control, or stress throughout the projects.

Another form of organizational support is project maturity. Project maturity refers to an organization's capability to support project execution. Team members were on the fence

Table 5.12: Synthesis of Results for Workload, Job Demands, Job Control, and Stress

	Hypothesis	Level of Support
5.1	Project workload, job demands, and stress will be positively related	Moderate support
5.2	Both measures of job control (i.e., decisional authority and skill discretion) will be positively related	Strong support
5.3	Project workload, job demands, and stress will be inversely related to job control	Mixed Results
5.4	Project workload, job demands, and stress should be positively related to anxiety and depression	Strong support
5.5	Job control should be negatively related to anxiety and depression	Strong to moderate support
5.6	Supporting infrastructure will be negatively related to project workload, job demands, and stress	No support
5.7	Supporting infrastructure will be positively related to job control	No support
5.8	Maturity will be negatively related to project workload, job demands, and stress	Moderate support
5.9	Maturity will be positively related to job control	Not supported
5.10	Project workload, job demands, and stress will be positively associated with social support	Moderate support
5.11	Job control will not be related to social support	Moderate support - Skill discretion positively correlated to attachment, opportunity for nurturance, reliable alliance, and guidance at T1, and social integration and opportunity for nurturance at T2.
5.12	Project workload, job demands, and stress will be negatively associated with collaboration	Weak to moderate support
5.13	Job control will be positively related to collaboration	Moderate support
5.14	People high on problem solving and high on forcing (i.e., high concern for self) will report less perceived job demands and less perceived stress	Mixed support
5.15	People high on problem solving and high on forcing (i.e., high concern for self) will report more control over their job	Mixed support
5.16	Project workload, job demands, and stress will be positively related to all forms of conflict	Moderate support
5.17	Job control will be positively related to all forms of conflict	Mixed support
5.18	Project workload, job demands, and stress will be positively related to task interdependency	Not supported
5.19	Job control will be positively related to task interdependence	Strong support
5.20	Project workload, job demands, and stress will be negatively related to goal clarity and goal similarity	Weak support
5.21	Job control will be positively related to goal clarity and goal similarity	Moderate support
5.22	Project workload, job demands, and stress will be negatively related to task proficiency, adaptive behaviors, and proactivity	Moderate support
5.23	Job control will be positively related to task proficiency, adaptive behaviors, and proactivity	Strong support
5.24	Project workload, job demands, and stress will negatively impact project performance	Weak support - Negative trends for demands and stress with Time and Budget performance.
5.25	Job control will positively impact project performance	Weak support - Positive trends for skill discretion with functional performance at T1.

in terms of this form of support, neither agreeing nor disagreeing benefiting from it. While project maturity did not seem to impact job demands, job control, and stress overall, a deeper examination of questionnaire items reveals some interesting results. Recall from Figure 1 that organizational support was assessed before project initiation. Interestingly, as early reports of concrete support from executives (such as understanding project management principles or things as simple as attending project team meetings) increased, job demands at time 2—that is, many weeks later when the project is well underway and being executed—decreased. Similarly, as reports of organizations having well-defined project management methodology, high commitment for up-front planning, and effort to minimize score "creep" increased, job demands at time 2 decreased.

Support can also be provided between members of a team. Of the 6 types of social support, socio-affective support such as opportunity for nurturance (i.e., the sense that others rely upon one for their well-being), attachment (i.e., emotional closeness from which one derives a sense of security), and social integration (i.e., a sense of belonging to a group that shares similar interests, concerns, and recreational activities) were those most related to job demands, job control, and stress. More tangible forms of support, such as guidance (i.e., provision of information and advice), reliable alliance (i.e., the assurance that others can be counted upon for tangible assistance), and reassurance of worth (i.e., recognition of one's competence, skills, and value by others) were generally not related to job demands, job control, and stress. Overall, the different forms of social support were positively related to job demands, job control, and stress. This suggests that as demands and stress increase, so does the importance of socio-affective support. This also suggests that decision authority and skill discretion increases are associated with socio-emotional support increases as well. However, caution must be exercised, as the instrument measuring social support appeared to lack internal consistency (see Appendix 9).

Collaboration

We expected, and generally found, that decisional latitude and, most importantly, skill discretion tend to be positively related with collaborative behaviors. However, contrary to our expectations, job demands and stress tended to be negatively related to collaborative behaviors.

Hence, it seems that for project team members in health care, while job control and interactions in the form of collaboration appear to go hand in hand (i.e., both affecting each other positively), collaboration can be considered an additional demand and a source of stress rather than something that is helpful. Another explanation could be that job demands and stress lessens team member's capability to collaborate.

Conflict

Conflict manifestations and the manner with which people tend to manage conflict are crucial for individual, team, and project performance. We found that everybody had some affinity with *all* forms of conflict handling. Because conflict management styles were measured at time 0 and job demands, job control, and stress were measures weeks and even months later at times 1 and 2, it is interesting to see how they relate to each other.

Overall, results suggest that skill discretion seem to result from a preference with problem-solving and making compromises. There are also indications that scoring high on imposing solutions on others is positively associated with decision authority. Also, we found that high scores on preference for making compromises tend to be positively related to job demands and negatively related to stress. The negative relation to stress is particularly salient in later stages of projects. In other words, the more people reported resorting to problem-solving "in general" before the project started, the less they felt stressed during project execution months later. These results suggest that preference for problem-solving is a stress reducer, presumably because conflicts tend to be managed more satisfactorily when this strategy is employed.

Although team members did not report frequent task, process, or relational conflicts, there were interesting trends involving project workload, job demands, job control, and stress. Project workload at time 1 is positively related to task conflict at times 1 and 2. In early stages of the project, job control tended not be related to relational or task conflict and to be negatively related to process conflict. Hence, as levels of decisional latitude and skill discretion increase, reported incidents of disagreements over how to proceed with the project decrease. Later however, while there was still no relationship with task conflict, these two components of job control were positively related to relational and process conflict. It seems that in early stages of a project, behaviors such as initiative taking and having the latitude to decide how to do one's job help reduce process conflict. In later stages, the same behaviors may contribute to relational and process conflicts.

In terms of job demands and stress, early project phases seem unimportant. Later however, things change. Both job demands and stress are positively related to occurrences of task and process conflict. This suggests that not having enough time to do everything, having to work fast, and having difficulties coping with workload would tend to increase occurrences of disagreements among teammates with what to do in the project and how to do it.

Performance

Examining the impact of job demands, job control, and stress on determinants of performance such as task interdependency and goal clarity/similarity reveals generally positive correlations with job control and negative ones with stress. Correlations between job control and all types of behavioral performance – task proficiency, adaptation, and proactivity– are positive. Correlations with job demands and stress are less numerous and generally negative. When examining the impact self-reported levels of job demands, job control, and stress on perceptions of project performance, our results are less sticking. The few results that stand out suggest that high demands and high stress are negatively related to time and budget performance and high skill discretion is positively related to regularly assessing the projects progression and functional performance. Overall, job demands, job control and stress impact determinants of job performance, job performance itself and to some extent, more distal issues pertaining to project success.

Chapter 6

Recognition, Autonomy and Power: A Qualitative Retrospective Examination

In the previous chapter, we focused our attention on demands and control, and, in the case of control, on decision authority and skill discretion. Although there is a strong research tradition on which these concepts take footing—mostly quantitative and positivist—there is room for additional perspectives. Indeed, we believe that the study of complex phenomena should benefit from a variety of research approaches and that this form of triangulation is, in fact, the sign of a healthy research endeavor. Accordingly, in this chapter we draw on similar constructs similar to demands, decision authority, and skill discretion; however, they stem from a qualitative and constructivist perspective.

The Psychodynamics of Work

Psychodynamics of work is a discipline influenced by ergonomics, psychoanalysis and sociology. First developed in France in the '70s (Dejours, 1980, 1994, 2000, 2009a, 2009b; Molinier, 2006), it now has roots in other European countries as well as in North America (Alderson, 2010; Brun, 1992; Carpentier-Roy, 1989; Carpentier-Roy & Vézina, 2000; Institut de psychodynamique du travail du Québec, 2006; Therriault, 2010; Trudel, 1999), and Brazil (Uchida, Sznelwar, & Lancman, 2011).

The theory takes footing on two sets of interrelated concepts. The first concept is that there is a gap between what people want to achieve and what gets achieved, and that this gap is both a source of "pleasure" and "pain." Second, the theory posits three vectors that account for meaning and sense-making at work: recognition, autonomy, and power. We will now turn to these concepts.

Working Towards Unmet Objectives as a Source of "Pleasure" and "Pain"

For Dejours (2000), work offers opportunities in the form of challenges to meet. The gap between what needs to be achieved and what gets to be achieved is the prompt that mobilizes one to engage in the collective effort through thought and inventiveness. As such, the process of bridging the gap and achieving results brings "pleasure"; that is, a state of happiness and content. A discombobulated process and unmet objectives can also bring "pain," leaving one despondent and dejected.

According to psychodynamics of work, teamwork is considered an activity character-ized by actions, know-how, and the mobilization of intelligence that enables the ability to think, interpret, and respond to situations. As such, the encounter between team members, their eagerness—or lack thereof—to engage and achieve the projects' objectives in spite of external constraints is the cornerstone of pleasure and pain at work.

One of the external constraints is the organization's capability to offer opportunities, or lack of opportunity, to bridge gaps have a direct influence on the experience of pleasure and pain (Alderson, 2004; Therriault, Rhéaume, & Streit, 2004; Vézina, 2000). Pain and suffering occurs when the organization or other team members thwarts oneself in his/her search for solutions, expression of creativity, and engagement in the process of problem solving. This creates a mental imbalance that is painful in itself and furthermore, that compromises one's ability to work towards meeting the objectives.

Davezies (2005) explains that collective work involves a dynamic mobilization of sub-jectivity and individual intelligence. When team members' intelligences fail to converge, conflicts arise and cohesion is destabilized or even compromised if external constraints are too rigid. When team members' intelligences converge, a transformative dynamic sets in and the team can carry out its project effectively. In such cases, team members learn to adjust to each other and the situation and establish an effective work organization condu-cive to cooperation and true collaboration. According to Dejours (2009b), this cooperation will foster collective discussions or deliberations leading to the establishment of social norms that structures the project and prompts the team to evolve. Deliberations and the establishment of norms structure the process of cooperation and serve as a binding agent and a common reference, promoting cohesion and collective regulation. As highlighted by Davezies (2010), working on a project team is more than just going through the motions—it is also the experience of togetherness, which requires commitment to each other and to the project to address conflicts that may arise from disagreements on how to complete the project.

Psychological Health as a Result of Recognition, Autonomy and Power

Carpentier-Roy (1995) describes suffering as what lies between psychological health and psychological illness, and further describes pain as a state of struggle faced by workers to avoid becoming ill. In teamwork, the manifestations of pain vary from one teammate to another and can take various forms such passivity, boredom, anger, or discouragement, but are rooted in two distinct causes: dissatisfaction and anxiety. Dissatisfaction—which occurs in the context of teamwork and is relevant to the task and its constraints—is often associated with a painful feeling of being frustrated in one's hopes and perceived entitlements. Anxiety is a perceived imbalance between outside threats and the intra-psychological means to deal with those threats. Anxiety can stem from the team's delib-erations, from the team's inability to manage its conflicts through social support, or it can come from external constraints. Threats can be real risks or risks that are suspected or imagined.

Three needs require satisfaction in order to foster pleasure and avoid pain and suffering. The first is the need for recognition. Recognition is a sign that others make sense of one's contribution in the attainment of collective and socially useful goals. In this sense, recognition is a determinant of self-fulfillment and contributes to building a positive self-image (Carpentier-Roy & Vézina, 2000; Dejours, 1994). Recognition offers a socially valued outcome to difficulties and problems encountered by team members in their attempts to meet objectives or in carrying out the task. As such, satisfying one's need for recognition generates meaning and pleasure at work. Non-recognition by others of one's contribution to the task and objectives can cause significant suffering. Non-recognition leads to self-doubt and loss of self-esteem. In the context of a team, the lack of recognition is often expressed by limiting the necessary authority and autonomy to perform one's assigned tasks.

Dejours (2000) states more specifically that recognition involves two types of judgments about the work: a judgment on utility, mostly expressed vertically (i.e., superiors-subordinates), and a judgment of beauty, mostly expressed horizontally (i.e., between peers). Both types of recognition judgments target the task. The judgment of utility confirms ones membership in the team and implies recognition in terms of the "what" that is in terms of conformity to agreed-upon standards. The judgment of beauty implies recognition in terms of "how" the task is carried out. It underscores one's uniqueness. Together, vertical and horizontal recognition binds different individuals through the pertinence and uniqueness of the task accomplishments.

The second need that requires satisfaction to foster pleasure and avoid pain and suffering is the need for power. Power refers to one's capability to decide, choose, and actually carry out the actions he/she is required to do. Power also implies understanding the scope and meaning of one's actions. Carpentier-Roy (1995) emphasizes that every person needs to control at least the acts for that he or she has developed skills and is accountable for.

Finally, autonomy is the third need that requires satisfaction. In work psychodynamic terms, autonomy refers to every worker's need to exercise control over the actions for which he or she has been trained and wishes to take responsibility for. Whereas power refers to the capability of doing, autonomy refers to how a person will act once power is satisfied. In a team and combined with professional identity, autonomy is reflected in the way the team members perform their duties. Because autonomy implies how one carries out tasks, it is a manifestation of creativity and innovativeness in one's capability in sustaining the teams operations and inner workings. For Carpentier-Roy (1995), power and autonomy are closely related to each other and to recognition.

Summary and Hypotheses

We have seen that pleasure and pain are a function of the gap between established and met goals. We also discussed how satisfying one's need for recognition, power, and autonomy leads to pleasure and how thwarting these needs leads to pain and suffering. We also maintained throughout that these concepts have tangible rooting in tasks and teamwork. Consequently, we will test the following hypotheses:

- Hy 6.1: Expressions of recognition, power, and autonomy should lead to pleasure.
- Hy 6.2: Expressions of lack recognition, power, and autonomy should lead to pain and suffering.

Method

Process

Our study process and timing of our measures are detailed in Figure 1 and Table 3.1.

Procedure

We chose to perform content analysis of end-of-project interviews to extract occurrences representative of our constructs. This allows us to move concrete manifestations to abstract concepts by identifying the essential characteristics of our phenomena of interest (Bardin, 1998).

Specifically, the analysis was mainly carried out from traces of oral interviews conducted with volunteer participants of the 11 project teams described previously. Interviews were covered by ethics reviews and were described in consent forms that project participants signed at the beginning of the project. As an additional precaution, at the beginning of the interview, all participants were informed of the risks associated with the process and voluntarily agreed to participate.

At least one member of each team and as many as six per team agreed to participate for a total of 49 (i.e., 60% of all team members). Interviews were performed by three trained research assistants using a standardized semi-structured interview protocol (see Appendix 4). Interviews were recorded and notes were taken. On average, interviews lasted about 38 minutes.

The first step involved the first three teams (see Table 3.2). Repeated readings of verbatim text aimed to bring out the greatest number of concepts and possible categories. It was thus possible to identify the major themes to explore: the sources of pleasure and pain arising from work in a project team and delivery of meaningful content of the task (recognition, power, and autonomy). Later we added the themes of cooperation, coexistence, and trust. These categories are based on our general knowledge and scientific literature on teams, professions, and interprofessional work, project management, and well-being, as well as personal experiences with health care teams. No restriction on the number of categories has been issued at this stage of data coding.

Interview data from subsequent teams were compared from one team to another by a cross-sectional analysis that allows the identification of sequences and thematic groupings. Gradually, by working back and forth between theory and empirical evidence from the interview material, a coherent representation of the results emerged.

Results

Positive impact of recognition, power and autonomy

Recognition

Recognition is an indication that others register and make sense of one's contribution. Manifestations of recognition abound in our interviews. The following excerpts are two examples.

> Excerpt 1. *I like how my colleague approached this phase of the project, it's effective and it allowed us to move faster.*

> Excerpt 2. *This colleague has a really unique way of doing things, his actions appear simple and effective.*

The first quote, coming from the leader of a team/project, is a good example of vertical recognition in the form of a judgment of utility. The second quote, coming from a peer, shows horizontal recognition in terms of a judgment of beauty. Both examples show specific and targeted recognition and are examples of what fosters togetherness.

Although frequent, recognition is not always as obvious, and its effect is not always the same across situations. In a project team, recognition is a testament to individuals' singular and socially useful contribution to the project endeavor. For example, in the following excerpts, it is shown how recognition, through the judgment of utility, can act on peoples' decisions to join the team in spite of the extra workload it involves (excerpt 3), on their level of support to the project (excerpt 4), and on their motivation to learn (excerpt 5).

Excerpt 3.   *I knew by agreeing to participate in this project it would give me more work, but I also knew with whom I was going to work. With these people, it is clear from the onset that it will go well, they are used to talking and helping each other. It makes it interesting from the get-go to work on this project.*

Excerpt 4.   *When I heard about the project, I agreed to support it immediately. I know the leader. Everyone wants to work with her. She is very dynamic and I know she can achieve results quickly.*

Excerpt 5.   *This person knows how to go about doing things, it seemed so easy, she knows her job. It's a great opportunity to rub shoulders in this project and take advantage of her expertise.*

Our data showed that recognition is key to teamwork as it contributes to the establishment of a climate of trust in which it is safe to discuss and deliberate among project team members. This climate is the basis for the construction of norms regarding roles (excerpt 6) as well as trust and commitment (excerpt 7).

Excerpt 6.   *Communication allowed us to quickly understand our roles in the project. Defining the project and further clarifying our respective roles advanced the project safely step-by-step. Now everyone has the same vision of the project.*

Excerpt 7.   *Trust in my colleagues is why I joined the team and offered my services; I knew with whom I was making a commitment with.*

The dynamics of recognition have traction as long as they take place within a system of rules and norms, and if they are regularly discussed and debated. These norms and discussions support taskwork and requirements of processes. They are also the basis of social bonds and a sense of belonging to the team. This sense of belonging is necessary for judgments of utility and beauty to operate through recognition.

Power

Our interview material clearly illustrated the importance of power, that is, the importance of one's capability to decide, choose, and carry out what one is supposed to do. For example:

Excerpt 8.   *Overall, I am more in the "doing" than in the "thinking." In the heat of things, you must work at your maximum all the time. I like that.*

In addition, we found that power exerted by the leader translated into positive persuasion. For example, excerpt 9 shows the impact of intellectual mobilization of one's subjective views across hierarchical divides.

> Excerpt 9.   *This person knows how to use the right arguments to make us adhere to his ideas.*

When intelligences converge, a common dynamic emerges from which true teamwork toward a common objective is possible. In these cases, a project team provides team members opportunities to experience power through the sharing of one's unique experiences (excerpt 10), something that is easier when there is a shared sense of togetherness (excerpt 11).

> Excerpt 10.   *I've always worked in teams, this is not the first project I'm on. You'll see, I'm going to share my experience and everything will be fine.*

> Excerpt 11.   *It's easier to work with people who are altruistic.*

Autonomy

Autonomy is reflected in the way people choose to perform their job. Autonomy is directly related to one's competency and disciplinary expertise. Excerpt 12 shows how respect for each others' autonomy is key, as well as related to recognition.

> Excerpt 12.   *In a team project, it is important to recognize and respect each other's differences and be able to work with different people.*

In teamwork, autonomy is required for any person to control the act for which he or she was trained and for which he or she wishes to be accountable for. As we discovered for recognition, manifestations of autonomy were commensurate with other phenomena such as learning of and adjusting to each others' contribution to the project (excerpt 13), and mutual trust during discussions (excerpts 14 and 15).

> Excerpt 13.   *We had to learn to know each other, what each participant could bring to the project, and how everyone could contribute. Also, working as a team implies a constant adjustment if we want this to work.*

> Excerpt 14.   *In team meetings, we do not feel judged on our contribution. All the ideas were good, they were discussed. We chose the best ideas, while respecting everybody. It's nice to work in that context.*

> Excerpt 15.   *Self-confidence is being able to say what you think. When there is an opening, it's easy to say what one thinks.*

As we can see, trust among team members has a positive effect on social relations. Furthermore, as excerpts 16 and 17 shows, our data hints at reciprocal interactions between open communications regarding committing to tasks and completing them, and fostering more autonomy by pinpointing additional tasks that are complementary.

> Excerpt 16.   *All those that committed to tasks completed them. In such a context, you feel like taking on more work.*

Excerpt 17. *By knowing more about my colleagues, I know more on what things I can trust them with and what I should take care of myself.*

Team members' manifestations of instances of autonomy were intertwined with the importance of respect with what people can bring that is unique. For example:

Excerpt 18. *A good collaboration is based on respect for each other's differences and strengths as well as consideration for skills and weaknesses.*

All three taken together

The weaving of task-related recognition, power, and autonomy shows that project work is more than simply coordinating tasks; it impacts team members and teamwork. All acts converge with intent to affect each team member. When things are going well, recognition, autonomy, and power promote an environment of mutual trust, commitment, and cooperation, which contributes to strengthen each individual place in the team. The resulting experience of pleasure draws on how one feels after his or her contribution is recognized. Framed in a positive way, the effects of recognition, autonomy, and power are driving the team members' commitment in the project team.

Excerpt 19. *Colleagues are very committed to each other. Each member carries out his task. When experiencing difficulties, we help each other a lot. When one of us has a small loss of energy, we offer encouragement.*

Excerpt 20. *At first, perceptions of the project were different, the vision was divergent, and the understanding of the objective was not the same. Now that we have discussed and shared out thoughts, we are able to hear each other out. We can still disagree on certain issues, but at least it is possible to have a consensus. From then on, we felt that we are able to move forward, all in the same direction.*

Negative Impact of Recognition, Power and Autonomy

Recognition

Our interview material was evocative of contexts, situations, and affects that co-occurred or overlapped with instances of lack of recognition. Excerpt 21 shows that lack of recognition during project execution can cause confusion.

Excerpt 21. *Managers never say if the project will be supported in the future. Also, they do not guarantee if people can remain on the team or will have the same functions.*

We also saw that lack of recognition can also cause negative affect (first part of excerpt 22). Moreover, lack of recognition reverberates in team dynamics and can enhance feelings of distance between team members (second part of excerpt 22). Such phenomena can lead to decreases in mental health.

Excerpt 22. *This attitude causes me a lot of disappointment, grief, and anger towards my colleagues.*

We saw in the previous section that in trusting climate, recognition promotes commitment to the project and the establishment of norms sustaining togetherness. In parallel, we consistently saw how lack of recognition was commensurate with the emergence of distrust (excerpt 23).

> Excerpt 23. *The manager, who I thought I trusted, did not support our requests for equipment. It's frustrating. These were not my personal demands; they were what the whole team demanded.*

Our exploration of the data suggests that when distrust emerged, negative affect hindered collective work and mobilization.

Power

Working with others requires making some compromises on how to do things. But making compromises exert a psychological toll. Excerpt 24 shows how difficult it is for some to make compromises and how such an attitude can lead to forcing one's solutions onto others.

> Excerpt 24. *If the project leader doesn't do his part, I'll do it for him. There's no time to wait around. This is what happened in my team. Since the person responsible for the project did not assert his leadership, I took over that role even though, strictly speaking, it was not my function. I did it to move the project forward, to tell others what to do and how to do it.*

When intelligences diverge, team dynamics consistent with reaching a common goal is thwarted. Project work requires that every team member understands each other's contribution to project objectives (excerpt 25). When team climate is unsupportive or when proper deliberations are hindered—often because of members' attitudes (excerpt 26)—people's actions are constrained. In turn, this limits their ability to choose and direct their actions toward the common goal.

> Excerpt 25. *The problem is that the team, the "we," consists of individuals who have different levels of responsibility and are not all equally available. That makes it difficult to get a "we" that is homogeneous and feel we really are a team that can carry out a project together.*

> Excerpt 26. *It's more difficult to work with people who are selfish or narcissistic. They want to first meet their personal needs and will sometimes interact with others in inconsistent ways. This creates a difficult climate.*

What emerges from our data is that lack of power negatively affects team members' capability to act and invest themselves. Recognition—which is necessarily specific to individuals, makes them stand out but at the same time enables them to decide how to manage interdependencies—is the vector through which people weighted down by a lack of power can overcome these group difficulties.

Autonomy

Health care project teams are comprised of people from different professions and disciplines. Levels of responsibility vary. Furthermore, some professionals are the sole providers of certain medical acts (e.g., diagnosing a disease) while other medical acts can be shared between professions (e.g., injecting a vaccine, detecting high blood pressure, and adjusting the dose of a medication for hypoglycemia). These issues permeate health care ongoing service delivery, but as the excerpt 27 shows, it also appears in the context of a project work.

Excerpt 27. *We all want to participate in the team and express our views based on our respective experience or expertise. But since we do not all have the same level of authority, I think it can affect the expression of our expertise in the team.*

Furthermore, authority and hierarchy may inject confusion in project work and limit people's ability to do what they need to do (excerpt 28), affect the nature of the tasks to perform (excerpt 29), or even create aversion for certain tasks (excerpt 30).

Excerpt 28. *As a team, we must be open. We have the right to say what we think, to share ideas. We are not spectators, we are really actors. On the one hand, we are told that we must participate in the development of the project; on the other hand, it seems that it makes us do things we should not do.*

Excerpt 29. *In the team, there are too many "chiefs" and too few "Indians." What I mean is that there are too many managers. We are not enough to actually do the dirty work and if we don't do it, it just won't get done. It's not fair.*

Excerpt 30. *If there are new tasks to perform, I run away so I'm not forced to do them.*

All three taken together

These results show that there is real potential for project work to negatively affect the extent to which one's needs for recognition, power, and autonomy are satisfied. In such cases, people feel others are not aware of—and therefore cannot appreciate—their efforts and contribution (excerpt 31) and their latitude in putting forth their task-related skills is constrained (excerpt 32). Consequently, interprofessional collaboration itself is threatened through difficulties with interdisciplinary translations (excerpts 34) or worse, as it can be considered as not being part of the work (excerpt 35).

Excerpt 31. *We should have more opportunities to discuss our values, our interests, our strengths, our expectations, our frustrations, our anger. We could meet outside of our formal meetings to work together.*

Excerpt 32. *In my team, there was very little room for flexibility. I was too focused on project performance.*

Excerpt 33. *It was very demanding for me to bear all the conflicts, all this tension. I realize it now, because I am no longer part of the project; I feel that I finally found my freedom.*

Excerpt 34. *I feel the need to make an extra effort to translate each other's reality of each other.*

Excerpt 35. *It's clear to me that in the future, I will not get involved in a project. I'll just do my job—no more.*

Table 6.1: Synthesis of Results for Qualitative Results.

Hypothesis	Level of Support
6.1 Expressions of recognition, power, and autonomy should lead to pleasure.	Moderate support
6.2 Expressions of lack recognition, power, and autonomy should lead to pain and suffering.	Strong support

Results Summary and Preliminary Discussion

We initiated our analysis on the basis of two hypotheses. The first predicted that satisfying people's need for recognition, power, and autonomy fosters experiences of pleasure, and by extension, fosters healthy psychological states. The second predicted that when recognition, power and autonomy are thwarted, people experience pain and suffering and consequently have less psychological health, possibly even psychological illness. Table 6.1 summarizes the results.

While our retrospective qualitative data do not go as far as suggesting a clear relation with psychological health, results do, however, suggest that experiences of pleasure co-occur with felt recognition and the required space to exercise power as well as the necessary leeway to experience autonomy. These phenomena energize individuals toward goal accomplishments and foster trust in teams.

In parallel, when recognition, power and autonomy are denied or constrained, negative affects appear and require energy that, instead of being used to meet project objectives, is used to mount defensive strategies to wrestle against pain and suffering. In turn, pain and suffering limits one's ability to perceive recognition, accentuates volitional constraints, and adds limitations over the very actions one has been trained to do.

Chapter 7

Addressing Paradoxes of Interprofessional Health Care Project Teams

Overview and Summary of Results

Collaboration is now recognized as the centerpiece of quality health care delivery (Frank, 2005) because the practice and science of health care delivery has become too complex to rely on archaic individual decision-making processes and actions. This dramatic change is occurring in health care facilities, innovative graduate and continuous training programs, and certification boards by aligning their efforts to train and educate health care professionals to the benefits of patient-centered interprofessional collaboration (Boucher, Chaput, Ste-Marie, & Millette, 2008). The endeavor is challenging, however, because of the natural resistance to new ways of doing things. Furthermore, in addition to the lack of project management awareness, interprofessional collaboration is only seen as an aid to "regular" ongoing service delivery work and not as a key ingredient to project success. This book was written to address this issue and the complex paradoxes interprofessional health care project teams face.

In our view, the challenges facing interprofessional health care project teams can be summarized into five paradoxes. First, although it might seem simple at first glance, collaborating across professional silos is actually a complex array of intertwined phenomena – giving voice and translating one's knowledge and expertise, and integrating others' knowledge and expertise – which are not effective if only fueled by common sense or intuition. Second, good collaborative skills and sound collaborative practices are required to improve interprofessional collaboration; consequently, one is thwarted without the other. Third, because of the nature of the work performed in health care (i.e., ongoing service delivery) and the keenness of professionals to strive for constant progress, health care workers are eager to engage in continuous improvement initiatives. Yet, if continuous improvement initiatives are effective, they have not diminished the need to improve on interprofessional collaboration, and if they are ineffective, an alternative is needed. Fourth, whether they know they are involved in a project or not, health care workers are largely unaware of a valuable alternative – that is, they are unaware of the contribution project management can make in bringing about a radical change initiative. Hence, this managerial "blind spot" compounds usual difficulties of interprofessional collaboration because it is difficult to translate knowledge and expertise across professional knowledge silos in a way commensurate with project success. The fifth paradox is that a successful project completion is dependent upon resolving all previous paradoxes. These paradoxes imply that interprofessional collaboration is a difficult and far-reaching challenge, and consequently, exerts a toll on the health of health care workers involved in projects and severely hinders project success.

These complex problems have motivated us to study workload, job demands, job control, and stress in the context of interprofessional health care project teams, which we did using validated quantitative questionnaires and qualitative interviews (for details on our study's limitations, see Appendix 9).

Training Efficacy

Our training program was built on four criteria (i.e., comprehensiveness, specificity, just-in-time and relatedness) and three core principles (i.e., acquiring and maintaining a clear understanding of the outcome and process of the project; uncertainty, planning, and control as integral elements of project work; and the importance of individual, team, and stakeholder drivers being monitored and understood throughout the project). But perhaps more importantly, our training program was built on our belief that interprofessional collaboration and project management are intimately intertwined, and that training on only one aspect is not sufficient.

Participants were satisfied with our program and felt they were being transferred needed knowledge and skills. Self-efficacy gains (i.e., the difference between pre- and post-workshop capability beliefs) show increases in both the human and project management components of our program. Interestingly, some measures of training efficacy seem to have worsened perceptions of job demands, job control, and stress, especially in the early stages of projects (in later stages, training efficacy is, as expected, related to decreasing levels of stress). Because of the "blind spot" we mentioned earlier, it is possible that awakening health care workers to the challenges of interprofessional collaboration in the context of project management might have created a temporary surge of job demands and stress and a decreased sense of job control. Although apparently contradictory in terms of the overall effect our training program should elicit, we believe this is a normal phenomenon when examining it through the lens of team adaptation and the role of situational awareness. Burke, Stagl, Salas, Pierce, & Kendall (2006) explain that for teams to adapt, team members must first scan their environment and become aware of the opportunities and threats of their situation, then share this awareness among each other. This, in turn, is followed by planning, executing, and learning. Given participants were largely unaware of the intricacies of interprofessional collaboration in the context of a project, and equally unaware of project management principles, our training may have temporarily triggered participants' awareness of the challenges of collaboration and project management early in the project.

The program had the most impact on increasing individuals' perceptions of some dimensions of collaboration in their teams and on decreasing somewhat self-reports of conflict behaviors. Often, this impact spanned weeks, even months, between the time health care workers participated in the workshops and the time outcome measures were taken.

The program had apparently no impact on behavioral performance and limited impact on project success. However, it is conceivable that the program's impact on collaboration and conflict indirectly affected project performance. This is because collaboration is a known predictor of team performance (Kozlowski & Bell, 2003; Kozlowski et al., 1999) and of project success (Chiocchio, 2007; Chiocchio, Forgues, et al., 2011; Hoegl et al., 2004). In addition, high conflict is related to reduced team performance (De Dreu & Weingart, 2003). Hence, since our program positively affected collaboration and negatively affected conflict, it is possible that it also impacted performance. Given our objective in this book – provide a description of phenomena using simple univariate statistics – it is not possible to examine the impact of complex multivariate mediation processes.

Another issue might have prevented us from detecting the impact of our training program. Overall self-efficacy gains, whether for human factors or project management factors, did not produce many noteworthy correlations with other study variables. This is disappointing since capability beliefs have a long history of being related to action (Bandura, 1977, 1982, 1986, 1997). However, we posit that our manipulation of original scores provided by participants into a difference score was problematic. Asking participants to self-report capability beliefs using learning objectives framed as actionable behaviors in terms of human and project management issues is not in question. But, our later manipulation of these measures into gain indices by subtracting post-workshop measures from pre-workshop measures may have reduced our capacity to detect the true impact of self-efficacy (see Edwards, 2001, for a discussion on problems with difference scores). An alternative would have been to use polynomial regression techniques (Edwards, 1994; Edwards, Cable, Williamson, Lambert, & Shipp, 2006; Edwards & Parry, 1993). However, these complex statistical models require a large number of participants (which we do not have; see Appendix 9) and are beyond the scope of the univariate statistics we chose to use.

Project Workload, Job Demands, Job Control, and Stress from Quantitative and Qualitative Perspectives

Quantitative results

Project work exerts a toll on the psychological health of health care workers. The Project Involvement Index is between 21 and 22, and correlates positively with job demands decision authority within and between times. It also correlates positively with decision authority at time 2. Skill discretion and decision authority are forms of control that are inversely related to anxiety and depression, such as increasing levels of job control being associated with decreasing measures of mental health.

Organizational support does not seem to have an impact on job control, which it should. Although social support measures are not necessarily internally consistent, results suggest skill discretion is the strongest predictor of most forms of social support. In parallel, of all the social support measures, social integration (i.e., a sense of belonging to a group that shares similar interests, concerns, and recreational activities) at time 2 is positively related to project involvement, decision authority, and skill discretion at both times.

Skill discretion is directly related to teamwork communication, synchrony, implicit coordination, and interprofessional collaboration, but mostly at time 1. In parallel, stress may have contributed to stifle peoples' collaborative behaviors, especially later in the project.

Conflict management measures show that making compromises and problem-solving are the strategies that correlate the most with job demands (positively), job control (positively), and stress (negatively).

For the most part, increased project workload, job demands, job control, and stress are all related to more conflict manifestations. This suggests that increased pressure and more conflict behaviors go together. Moreover, it also suggests that job control – if and how health care workers perform their project-related duties – is also positively associated to more frequent conflicts.

How team members interact in terms of their tasks is important, since skill discretion and decision authority are positively related to task interdependency. Also, augmentations of job control seem to correspond to increased levels of goal clarity and goal similarity.

Although job demands and stress do not relate overwhelmingly with performance behaviors, project involvement seems to increase various indices of proficiency, adaptivity, and proactivity. This suggests that high levels of project activity stimulate individuals' performance behaviors. Interestingly, decision authority and skill discretion is consistently related to proficiency, adaptivity, and proactivity.

Overall, project involvement, demands, control, and stress do not seem to hold strong with many relationships with various measures of project performance.

Qualitative results

Qualitative results show that manifestations of recognition, power, and autonomy create conditions favoring pleasurable states. That portion of the study also shows that when recognition, power, and autonomy are limited and stifled, people report negative affects and express suffering. Pleasurable states invigorate individuals towards goal accomplishments and create a trusting climate. In parallel, pain and suffering spiral into distrust and resentment.

Bridges between two theoretical models and approaches

Studies are often conducted within the confines of two parallel theoretical and methodological positions. One stems from a positivist perspective and uses quantitative data to describe, understand, and predict phenomena. Another uses a constructivist perspective and qualitative data to advance knowledge. We believe it is necessary for scientists to design studies that build on both traditions to engage in scientific discovery – doing so is a commitment to triangulation.

From a theoretical and conceptual point of view, the relationships among demand-control-support theory (Karasek & Theorell, 1990), effort-reward imbalance model (Siegrist, 1996), and work psychodynamics (Dejours, 2000) share similarities. First, control's decision authority and work psychodynamics' power are similar constructs: both imply that an individual requires latitude to decide what to do. Second, control's skill discretion and work psychodynamics' autonomy are both defined as people's capacity to decide how to enact their task-related behaviors. Third, work psychogynamics relates recognition to positive outcomes similarly with Siegrist (1996), who suggests that people's social roles at work provide opportunities for self-efficacy, self-esteem, and relatedness, as long as social exchanges are reciprocal and fair. While work psychodynamics discusses pain and suffering as a result of lack of recognition, power, and autonomy, the effort-reward imbalance perspective postulates that high effort accompanied with low reward is stressful and causes adverse health outcomes because people expect reciprocity from other actors in their social environment.

In addition, data is consistent between theories and methods. For example, health care workers report moderate to high quantitative levels of project involvement and job demands, while excerpt 3 suggests people are aware of the fact that project work is demanding and excerpt 19 refers to lack of energy. Quantitative levels of teamwork communication, goal clarity, and goal similarity find echoes in qualitative excerpts that testify of people's efforts to discuss roles and foster common understanding among the team (i.e., excerpts 6, 9, 12, 14, 20). Quantitative measures of adaptive and proactive performance behaviors relate well to interview material of people expressing the need for continuous adjustment (i.e., excerpt 13). Excerpts 14 and 20 hint at problem-solving, given a propensity to demonstrate a concern for others. Excerpt 16 discusses commitment decisions to perform tasks, which is in essence what decision authority relates to. And excerpt 19 also discusses the importance of encouragements which relates well to opportunity for nurturance, a dimension of social support. Excerpt 24 is a good example of high decision authority and a propensity for resolving conflict through forceful imposition. Interestingly, our quantitative data show that decisional authority and a forceful style of conflict management are positively correlated.

Practical Implications

Competencies in Interprofessional Collaboration

Competency models are the backbone of university curriculums and continuous education. Historically, but at an increasing rate in recent times, governmental bodies and professional associations have gone to great pains to provide competency frameworks to help universities teach and assess interprofessional collaboration. Great efforts have been invested so that competency models can help professionals in place monitor and improve on their interprofessional collaboration practices.

For example, in 2009, six U.S. associations of schools of the health professions, including the Association of American Medical Colleges, came together to encourage and promote meaningful interprofessional education. In 2010, they jointly convened an expert panel of educators from medicine, dentistry, nursing, osteopathic medicine, pharmacy, and public health to develop core competencies for interprofessional collaborative practices. The panel's recommendations (see Schmitt, Blue, Aschenbrener, & Viggiano, 2011) specify four interprofessional core competencies and corresponding general competencies: values and ethics for interprofessional practice, roles and responsibilities, interprofessional communication, and teams and teamwork.

In Canada, the *Interprofessionnal Health Education Accreditation Standards Guide* was developed by the Accreditation of Interprofessional Health Education (2011) to provide suggestions for accreditation agencies to take into account when developing, implementing, and assessing interprofessional health education standards for accreditation purposes. Several Canadian professional associations were involved in the production of this guide.

In addition, the Royal College of Physicians and Surgeons of Canada published in 2005 the *CanMEDS 2005 Physician Competency Framework* (Frank, 2005), which oriented specialized medical training programs in Canada toward the development of seven roles for the future physician, one of which was that of collaborator. Frank adds "As collaborators, physicians effectively work within a health care team to achieve optimal patient care." (2005, p. 4) These seven roles coalesce into two key competencies. First, participating effectively and appropriately in an interprofessional health care team. Second, effectively working with other health professionals to prevent, negotiate, and resolve interprofessional conflict.

In parallel, a working group of the Canadian Interprofessional Health Collaborative (2010) developed an *Interprofessional Competency Framework*. Six competency domains highlight the knowledge, skills, attitudes and values that should shape interprofessional collaboration practices: interprofessional communication, patient/client/family/community-centered care, role clarification, team functioning, collaborative leadership, and interprofessional conflict resolution.

While these efforts to address ongoing service delivery are commendable and necessary, all are focused on improving ongoing service delivery. None, to our knowledge, address specifically the challenges of interprofessional collaborative practices pertinent to project work. As stated previously, project work is, by definition, the only way to purposefully implement radical changes.

> **Recommendation 1.** Integrate project management competencies in health care competency profiles.

While many project management competency models exist already (see for example Edum-Fotwe & McCaffer, 2000; Project Management Institute, 2002; Stretton, 2006), much work will be needed to uphold this recommendation. This is because there are many schools of thought regarding project management, with, at one end, a classical approach derived from engineering (see Project Management Institute, 2003, 2008), and a newer approach where project management itself is flexible and adaptive to change (Wysocki, 2009). Nonetheless, most project management approaches and competencies espouse a technical approach, which we feel is not sufficient to ensure project success.

Project Management in Interprofessional Health Care Project Teams: Impossible Without Addressing "Human Factors"

Project work is transient, temporary, and focuses on the organization and its inter-related subsystems. Project work differs from the enacting of expertise in ongoing contexts. Results from Chiocchio et al. (2010) and results presented here clearly show that professionals in health care are concurrently involved in two to four projects. Yet, university programs do not teach project management for health care workers in general and professionals in particular. Furthermore, handbooks we examined that target the health care community devote only a few pages to project management, and when they do, the focus is on technical issues (see Burns et al., 2012; Grieshaber, 1997). We based our approach on core project management principles (i.e., Table 4.2) that, while not avoiding the issue of project management tools and techniques, did not focus on them either. Hence, we feel it is necessary to list these recommendations:

Recommendation 2. Add project management curriculum to university health sciences programs.

Recommendation 3. Ensure project management teaching is based on core principles, rather than on learning how to use project management tools and techniques.

We also believe that continuous education for health care workers already in place would benefit from project management training. We have shown here that our training program, consisting of three three-hour workshops with the use of various templates, was effective. Self-efficacy gains were positive, which suggests participants felt an increase in capability beliefs after each workshop. Also, participants were very much in agreement that the training was satisfactory and that valuable knowledge and skill were transferred. Hence, we recommend that, in addition to implementing recommendation 3, others should also:

Recommendation 4. Integrate project management training for health care workers engaged in continuous education.

Our training program was based on four criteria (i.e., Table 4.1). Our data, but also discussions with trainees, suggest these served as a solid foundation. We believe it is the result of our dedication to interprofessional collaboration as we were ourselves members of an interprofessional team. As such, we co-developed and co-delivered the training, which was greatly appreciated. Consequently, we recommend others:

Recommendation 5. Ensure that criteria of comprehensiveness, specificity, just-in-time, and relatedness serve as the fundamental criteria for design and delivery of continuous education training.

Whether project management is taught in university settings or on-site to seasoned health care workers, the following recommendations should be taken into consideration.

Project management should integrate the "human factor." For example, although our training program did not impact performance directly, it did impact behaviors that are known to predict performance, such as collaboration and conflict. In turn, collaboration and conflict are key issues in all teams, including project teams (Chiocchio, Forgues, et al., 2011). Qualitative data are eloquent as to the importance of team dynamics. Hence, logically, we propose to:

Recommendation 6. Ensure that project management training includes content devoted to team interactions such as collaboration, conflict, and conflict management.

Although our program did not include a stress management component and did not have discussions or exercises on psychological health issues, our results clearly show that stress and anxiety- and depressive-like moods are facts of life among health care workers in our sample and that of Chiocchio et al. (2010). Coping skills to deal with high project involvement and high job demands are necessary.

> **Recommendation 7.** Ensure project management training includes content devoted to team stress and psychological health management.

Coping with stress and psychological health issues requires more than decision authority and skill discretion. Indeed, many discussions of challenges with project involvement revolved around difficulties with setting priorities and managing time. We wholeheartedly recommend to

> **Recommendation 8.** Ensure project management training includes content devoted to increase priority-setting skills and time management.

In short, the efficacy of our training program is promising in terms of continuous improvements. Furthermore, project management education can – and in our opinion, should – be part of the curriculum of health care disciplines.

Project Management: More that Individual and Team Sustainability

While it is obviously pertinent to recommend dealing with teaching, continuous education, and all that contributes to individuals and teams becoming more efficient, it is not sufficient. Organizations need some help too. Hence,

> **Recommendation 9.** Organizations must build and maintain their capacity to provide all the support and infrastructure required for their interprofessional health care project teams to successfully manage their projects.

The process of building project management maturity will be slower or even impossible as long as the culture in health care institutions overemphasizes quick fixes and immediate results (Tucker & Edmondson, 2003). Building project management capability is also an opportunity to have managers and health care workers work in tandem. The result of this process – efficacious support for managing projects management – will help in many ways, including fostering positive perceptions of organizational support. Our results show that many measures of project maturity are inversely related to project involvement and job demands – a factual measure of project workload, and a subjective one, respectively. In turn, we also showed that as perception of job demands increase, so do feelings of anxiety and depression. These are not trivial matters.

Future Research
Program Evaluation

In the last decades, universities have progressively aimed at implementing interprofessional education. However, as stressed by Reeves et al., "The research evidence for interprofessional education (IPE) has significantly evolved over the past decade, yet due to its inherent complexity, a clear understanding of its effects (i.e., on learner behavior, professional practice and patient care) is not yet fully within our grasp." (2010, pp. 230–231).

In addition to continuing efforts to study interprofessional collaboration education program, we believe:

Recommendation 10. Academics should initiate research programs aimed at evaluating educational programs jointly addressing project management and interprofessional collaboration.

A More Balanced Approach to Research on Psychological Health

Since 1946, the World Health Organization has defined health not only as the absence of illness, but rather as a state with gradations ranging from poor to good health (World Health Organization, 1946). Moreover, psychological health is viewed as a multidimensional construct including independent negative and positive manifestations (Achille, 2003). The positive side, called psychological well-being, has only recently been given scientific attention. In this sense, several definitions and conceptualizations have been proposed by researchers (Danna & Griffin, 1999), but two stand out: the hedonic and eudemonic conceptualizations of psychological well-being (Ryan & Deci, 2001).

The hedonic approach states that well-being is the subjective happiness experienced by an individual, which stems from physical and/or psychological pleasure (and displeasure) (Diener, Gohm, Suh, & Oishi, 1998; Kubovy, 1999). Thereby, the more pleasure experienced, the more optimal the level of happiness. Pleasure can be generated by the attainment of goals or results that are judged as important by an individual, whatever they may be. A person experiencing well-being, in this context, would be defined as satisfied with their lives if they feel a higher level of positive emotions than negative ones (Kahneman, Diener, & Schwarz, 1999). Several authors associated with the eudemonic stream have rejected the idea of subjective well-being as the principal criterion for well-being (Ryan & Deci, 2001). These same authors felt that the satisfaction of one's needs or the attainments of desired outcomes, even if they lead to pleasure, don't necessarily lead to well-being. According to Waterman (1993), well-being resides more in the fact of living one's life in accordance with one's self (or true self) and the pursuit of activities that correspond to our own cherished values. In this sense, well-being resides in the realization of one's full potential (Ryff, 1995), and is comprised of six main dimensions: autonomy, personal growth, self-acceptance, a sense of purpose in life, a sense of mastery of one's environment, and positive affiliations (Ryff & Keyes, 1995).

Even if the debate between these two approaches remains unresolved, it is more and more accepted by tenants of each of the two schools of thought that a more just vision of well-being would include both of the aforementioned streams (Diener et al., 1998; Keyes & Lopez, 2002) within a unique multidimensional construct of psychological well-being.

A growing interest on the subject of well-being has lead certain authors to adapt this concept to the particular context of the workplace. Consequently, psychological well-being at work would consist of, on one hand, job satisfaction, and on the other, the prevalence of positive emotions at work.

To date, few studies have specifically examined the effects of psychological well-being at work. Interest in the happy-productive worker hypothesis, however, supplied a number of studies. In fact, many reported a positive effect of psychological well-being at work on employee performance (Wright & Bonett, 1997; Wright, Bonett, & Sweeney, 1993; Wright

& Cropanzano, 2000). The presence of positive affect at work was also positively related to the evaluation by colleagues of the assistance provided by individuals (Lee & Allen, 2002), job satisfaction (Connolly & Viswesvaran, 2000), the issue of organizational citizenship behaviors (e.g., providing assistance to a colleague) (Hurtz & Donovan, 2000), and a reduced intention to leave employment (Van Katwyk, Fox, Spector, & Kelloway, 2000). According to a longitudinal study conducted by Pelled & Xin (1999), the presence of positive affect at work has also been linked to reduced absenteeism five months later. In addition, Lyubomirsky, King, and Diener (2005) reported, in an analysis of ten longitudinal studies measuring the prevalence of positive emotions as well as job performance, an average of .27 longitudinal correlation between these two variables. In another study, the presence of positive affect at work was negatively related to burnout (Thoresen, Kaplan, Barsky, Warren, & de Chermont, 2003). More negatively, feelings of depression, loss of self-esteem, hypertension, alcoholism, and drug use have all been linked to impaired well-being at work (Ivancevich & Matteson, 1980).

The effects of psychological well-being on workgroup processes are not yet well understood. A noteworthy study on health care teams by Garman, Corrigan & Morris (2002) posited that burnout is a construct detectable at the group level, and that it is negatively related to the level of satisfaction of patients under care. In another study on interprofessional teams in oncology, researchers found that 25% of teams reported high levels of emotional exhaustion, and that team leaders (invariably surgeons) and nurses scored highest (Catt, Fallowfield, Jenkins, Langridge, & Cox, 2005).

This rich discussion leads us to strongly suggest that, although there are no doubts project work can exert negative influences on people's stress and mental health:

> **Recommendation 11.** Future studies should focus on a more comprehensive view of mental health in general and its potential positive impacts in the context of project work in health care settings.

Based on some of Chiocchio at al.'s (2010) conclusions on distress and psychological well-being, examining the positive impact of project work could be done by comparing workers involved in projects in projectized and non-projectised organizations. While in projectized organizations, more projects could be perceived as adding unwanted workload, involving people usually occupied with service or production work (i.e., work usually done in non-projectized organizations) in a project could be perceived positively, removing workers from routine work, thus fostering autonomy and job satisfaction.

Testing for More Complex Hypotheses

One of this book's objectives was to provide initial evidence on the many issues that have an impact on health care workers involved in project work. Although we established a valuable foundation for interprofessional health care project teams, human resource practitioners, and project management offices in health care institutions to build on, given the paucity of data on the issue, our univariate and descriptive focus is only a beginning. Hence:

> **Recommendation 12.** Academics should conduct applied research with health care project teams on complex interactions of demands-control-support theory.

In a nutshell, the demands-control-support theory "is essentially a three-way interactive model. It proposes that the two-way interaction hypothesized by the demands-control model is further bounded by social support. Specifically, the model proposes that the moderating effects of control on the demand-strain relationship will be found *only* when support is high." (Bliese & Castro, 2000, p. 66, emphasis in the original).

Two streams of studies have examined the role social support plays in the demands-control-support model. The first considered the direct effect of social support on job performance. These studies look at the "iso-strain hypothesis" and posit that high–demand—low control/low–support jobs result in the highest incidence of health problems (Akerboom & Maes, 2006; Van Der Doef et al., 2000). According to this view, tangible social support has two main effects: it can act directly on stressors by lowering their effect, or act directly on strain by bridging the gap between high demands and low control (Jex, 1998). Studies testing the iso-strain hypothesis have generated mixed results, some supportive of the hypothesis, others not.

The second stream of studies, although more complex to carry out, examined the indirect effect of social support—the "buffering hypothesis." This hypothesis posits that high control and high social support buffers—that is, protects or counteracts—the negative effects of high job demands (Akerboom & Maes, 2006). Unfortunately, like the iso-strain hypothesis, the buffering hypothesis also received mixed results in health studies (Van Der Doef et al., 2000) and especially confusing results in occupational settings (S Cohen & Wills, 1985). For example, in a large Norwegian sample of the working population, researchers could confirm the iso-strain hypothesis, since the higher the demands and the lower the control and support, the higher were the anxiety and depression levels. However, these researchers did not find support for the buffer effect of support on strain, since people with intermediate levels of support had higher anxiety and depression scores compared to those with lower and higher support, or for control on demands, since for all levels of control, anxiety, and depression, scores decreased by decreasing demands levels, and for all levels of demands, anxiety, and depression, scores decreased by increasing control levels (Sanne et al., 2005).

Concluding Remarks

Project Work: True Transdisciplinary Collaboration?

D'Amour et al. (2005) put forth a taxonomy of collaboration in health care teams. In their framework, multidisciplinary collaboration entails juxtaposing knowledge and expertise between collaborators. Interdisciplinary collaboration requires knowledge and expertise to be translated across disciplinary boundaries and then integrated by others. Transdisciplinary collaboration implies boundaries have vanished. How can we make disciplinary boundaries vanish?

We believe interprofessional health care project teams offer a context and opportunities for disciplinary boundaries to vanish. Most of the movement toward better health care services originates in the dissatisfaction and inadequacies of multidisciplinary work. Indeed, limiting decision-making and problem-solving by adding each other's perspectives is not sufficient to address real-world complexities. To tackle the challenges of ongoing health care service delivery, health care workers must morph into interdisciplinary teams. However, interdisciplinarity is curtailed by the professionalization of health care. Indeed, when delivering health care services to patients, people from certain professions have more power and more decisional authority over their own work and over that of others from different professions. An overemphasis on hierarchy and misplaced deference to authority thwarts meaningful discussions on patient care (Henriksen & Dayton, 2006), and when people do not feel free to discuss sensitive issues, many problems follow, including performance problems (Souba et al., 2011). We believe project work changes this unhealthy dynamic. Project work can have this effect because a project's objective is not to heal patients, but to fix the system. In fixing the system,

- There are no protected medical acts or complex rules for shared medical acts;
- Teams include more than just health care workers (such as patients playing an active role in the change effort, administrative assistants, and managers), which makes collaboration more diversified;
- All are on equal footing in ensuring the system works;
- Since the solution is complex and ambiguous, the views and expertise of all is required.

Transdisciplinarity is the key to resolve the five embedded paradoxes we exposed in the beginning of this book. These paradoxes paralyze the health care sector from implementing radical change in the way health care workers interact with each other.

By knowingly forming a project team and knowingly using project management principles to fix the system, health care workers have an opportunity to step outside their usual positions and realize that diversified expertise and knowledge have equal footing in solving the problem of the project, which resolves the fourth paradox. By consciously sharing expertise and knowledge from the same perspective of equality with respect to the project objective and the complexity of its solution, project team members have an opportunity to engage in radical change and avoid relying on "stepping up" continuous improvements efforts, which resolves the third paradox. Conscious avoidance of the usual means of improving things – that is, avoidance of focusing on patients to gradually improve interprofessional collaboration – is an opportunity to refocus and aim at the real target, which is implement radical change in interprofessional collaboration itself; this resolves the second paradox. Finally, when people truly focus on the behaviors at the heart of collaboration, rather than relying on vague principles and intuition, they can embrace the challenges of task interdependency, decisional authority, skill discretion, adaptive behaviors, trust, conflict, and support; reflectively integrate what interprofessional collaboration is; and enact the required behaviors during the course of the project, which resolve the first paradox.

A First Step

We started this book with two quotations. Katz and Kahn's (1978) quotation eloquently shows the difficulties in trying to understand people who have a different frame of mind. As experts, we know a lot of things in our respective fields and can articulate this knowledge with considerable nuance. As we glance into a colleague's field, we see simple truths structured somewhat straightforwardly. One way around this is to work collaboratively.

But Klein's (2012) quotation sharply emphasizes that collaboration is not sufficient to exchange knowledge across disciplines. Both quotations are fairly pessimistic, as they state the problem but do not dwell on the solutions.

We conducted our study as an exploration of the problem of workload, stress, demands, and control in the context of interprofessional health care project teams. We wrote this book as an attempt to unearth solutions. Because of the paucity of studies on this particular type of team, we feel both our efforts at describing the problems and at generating solutions lack nuance. For the same reason however, we feel confident our labor can serve as a firm foundation from which health care workers can take additional steps and ascend towards more successful projects, and for scientists to advance the understanding of interprofessional health care project teams' effectiveness.

References

Accreditation of Interprofessional Health Education (AIHPE). (2011). *Interprofessional health education accrediation standards guide*. Retrieved from www.aiphe.ca.

Achille, M. (2003). Définir la santé au travail. 1. La base conceptuelle d'un modèle de la santé au travail. [Defining health at work: 1. Conceptual basis of a model of health at work]. In R. Foucher, A. Savoie & L. Brunet (Eds.), *Concilier performance organisationnelle et santé psychologique au travail*. Montréal (Canada): Édition Nouvelles.

Adelman, L., Miller, S. L., Henderson, D., & Schoelles, M. (2003). Using Brunskikian Theory and a Longitudinal Design to Study how Hierarchical Teams Adapt to Increasing Levels of Time Pressure. *Acta Psychologica, 112*, 181–206.

Akerboom, S., & Maes, S. (2006). Beyond demand and control: The contribution of organizational risk factors in assessing the psychological well-being of health care employees. *Work & Stress, 20*(1), 21–36.

Alderson, M. (2004). La psychodynamique du travail et le paradigme du stress: une saine et utile complémentarité en faveur du développement dans le champ de la santé au travail. *Santé mentale au Québec, 29*, 261–280.

Alderson, M. (2010). Analyse psychodynamique du travail infirmier. Une enquête en psychodynamique du travail en Centre d'Hébergement et de Soins de Longue Durée : entre plaisir et souffrance. Sarrebruck, Germany: Éditions Universitaires Européennes.

Andersen, E. S., & Jessen, S. A. (2003). Project maturity in organisations. *International Journal of Project Management, 21*(6), 457–461. doi: 10.1016/s0263-7863(02)00088-1

Arnetz, B. (2002). Organizational stress. In R. Ekman & B. Arnetz (Eds.), *Stress, Molecules, Individuals, Organization, Society*. Stockholm: Liber.

Ausubel, D. P. (1968). *Educational Psychology: A Cognitive View*. New York: Holt, Rinehart, and Winston.

Baker, E., Israel, B., & Schurman, S. (1996). Role of control and support in occupational stress: An integrated model. *Social Sceince & Medicine, 43*(7), 1145–1159.

Bandura, A. (1977). Self-efficacy: Toward a unifying theory of behavioral change. *Psychological Review, 84*(2), 191–215. doi: 10.1037/0033–295X.84.2.191

Bandura, A. (1982). Self-efficacy mechanism in human agency. *American Psychologist, 37*(2), 122–147. doi: 10.1037/0003-066X.37.2.122

Bandura, A. (1986). Social foundation of thought and action: A social cognitive theory. Englewood Cliffs, NJ: Prentice-Hall.

Bandura, A. (1997). *Self-efficacy — The exercise of control*. New York: W.H. Freeman and Company.

Bandura, A. (2006). Guide for construction self-efficacy scales. In T. Urdan & F. Pajares (Eds.), *Self-Efficacy Beliefs of Adolescents* (pp. 307–337). Charlotte, NC: Information Age Publishing.

Bardin, L. (1998). *L'analyse de contenu* (9 ed.). Paris: Presses Universitaires de France.

Beaulieu, G. (in progress). Développer le soutien aux besoins psychologiques des employés: Évaluation des effets cognitifs, affectifs, et comportementaux d'une formation destinée aux gestionnaires. Unpublished Ph.D. dissertation, Université de Montréal, Montréal, Canada.

Bedwell, W. L., Wildman, J. L., DiazGranados, D., Salazar, M., Kramer, W. S., & Salas, E. (2012). Collaboration at work: An integrative multilevel conceptualization. *Human Resource Management Review, 22*(2), 128–145. doi: 10.1016/j.hrmr.2011.11.007

Beehr, T. A., & Glazer, S. (2005). Organizational role stress. In J. Barling, E. K. Kelloway & M. R. Frone (Eds.), *Handbook of Work Stress* (pp. 7–33). Thoudand Oaks, CA: Sage.

Belout, A. (1998). Effects of human resource management on project effectiveness and success: Toward a new conceptual framework. *International Journal of Project Management, 16*(1), 21–26.

Bliese, P. D., & Castro, C. A. (2000). Role clarity, work overload and organizational support: Multilevel evidence of the importance of support. *Work & Stress, 14*(1), 65–73. doi: 10.1080/026783700417230

Borman, W. C., & Motowidlo, S. J. (1997). Task performance and contextual performance: The meaning for personnel selection research. *Human Performance, 10*(2), 99–109.

Borril, C., West, M., Shapiro, D., & Rees, A. (2000). Team working and effectiveness in health care. *British Journal of Health Care Management, 6,* 34–47.

Bosma, H., Marmot, M. G., Hemingway, H., Nicholson, A. C., Brunner, E., & Stansfeld, S. A. (1997). Low job control and risk of coronary heart disease in Whitehall II (prospective cohort) study. *BMJ, 314,* 558–565.

Boucher, A., Chaput, M., Ste-Marie, L. G., & Millette, B. (2008). *Changing the educational method to a Competency-Based Approach: Understanding the method before implementing the changes.* Paper presented at the Paper presented at the Royal College of Physicians and Surgeons of Canada annual meeting.

Bronstein, L. R. (2003). A model for interdisciplinary collaboration. *Social Work, 48*(3), 297–306.

Brown, J., Lewis, L., Ellis, K., Stewart, M., Freeman, T. R., & Kasperski, M. J. (2010). Conflict on interprofessional primary health care teams - can it be resolved? *Journal of Interprofessional Care, 25*(1), 4–10.

Brun, J.-P. (1992). Les hommes de lignes: analyse des phénomènes sociaux et subjectifs dans l'activité de travail des monteurs de lignes électriques Thèse de doctorat Ph.D., École Pratique des Hautes Études - Laboratoire d'ergonomie physiologique et cognitive, Paris, France.

Burke, C. S., Stagl, K. C., Salas, E., Pierce, L., & Kendall, D. (2006). Understanding team adaptation: A conceptual analysis and model. *Journal of Applied Psychology, 91*(6), 1189–1207. doi: 10.1037/0021-9010.91.6.1189

Burns, L. R., Bradley, E. H., & Weiner, B. J. (Eds.). (2012). *Shortell & Kaluzny's Health Care Management Organization Design & Behavior* (6 ed.). Delmar, NY: Cengage Learning.

Campion, A. C., Medsker, G. J., & Higgs, A. C. (1993). Relations between work group characteristics and effectiveness: Implications for designing effective work groups. *Personnel Psychology, 46,* 823–850.

Canadian Health Services Research Foundation. (2006). *Teamwork in healthcare: Promoting effective teamwork in healthcare in Canada*. Retrieved from www.chsrf.ca.

Canadian Interprofessional Health Collaborative. (2010). *A National Interprofessional Competency Framework*. Retrieved from http://www.cihc.ca.

Canadian Stroke Network. (2010). *Canadian Stroke Strategy: Canadian Best Practice Recommandations for Stroke Care*. Retrieved from http://canadianstrokestrategy.com/.

Carpentier-Roy, M.-C. (1989). Organisation du travail et santé mentale chez les infirmières en milieu hospitalier Ph.D., Université de Montréal, Montréal, Canada.

Carpentier-Roy, M.-C. (1995). Corps et âme : psychopathologie du travail infirmier (Deuxième édition augmentée) Montréal, Canada: Liber.

Carpentier-Roy, M.-C., & Vézina, M. (2000). *Le travail et ses malentendus - Enquêtes en psychodynamique du travail au Québec*. Québec, Canada: Les Presses de l'Université Laval.

Cartwright, D., & Zander, A. (1960). Group cohesiveness: Introduction. In D. Cartwright & A. Zander (Eds.), *Group dynamics: Research and theory*. New York: Harper Row.

Catt, S., Fallowfield, L., Jenkins, V., Langridge, C., & Cox, A. (2005). The informational roles and psychological health of members of 10 oncology multidisciplinary teams in the UK. *British Journal of Cancer 93*, 1092–1097.

Chiocchio, F. (2007). Project team performance: A study of electronic task and coordination communication. *Project Management Journal, 38*(1), 97–109.

Chiocchio, F. (2009). *Is the PMBOK® up to speed with HR issues? YES! (if you are a 1960's project manager)*. Paper presented at the PMI's Ottawa Valley Outaouais Chapter 9th annual symposium.

Chiocchio, F. (2011, Mai 2011). *Conflict and conflict asymmetry over time: the strange case of project teams*. Paper presented at the 15th Bi-Annual Conference of the European Congress of Work and Organizational Psychology.

Chiocchio, F., Beaulieu, G., Boudrias, J., Rousseau, V., Aubé, C., & Morin, E. (2010). The Project Involvement Index, psychological distress, and psychological well-being: Comparing workers from projectized and non-projectized organizations. *International Journal of Project Management, 28*(3), 201–211.

Chiocchio, F., Dubé, J.-N., & Lebel, P. (2012). *Initial validation evidence for a short self-reported scale measuring informational role self-efficacy* Paper presented at the 73rd Annual Canadian Psychological Association convention, Halifax (NS) Canada.

Chiocchio, F., & Forgues, D. (2008). Le rôle des objets-frontières dans l'apprentissage et la performance d'équipes d'étudiants travaillant à la conception de bâtiments durables [The role of boundary objects in learning and project team performance of students working on the design of sustainable buildings]. *Revue internationale des technologies en pédagogie universitaire, 5*(3), 6–21.

Chiocchio, F., Forgues, D., Paradis, D., & Iordanova, I. (2011). Teamwork in integrated design projects: Understanding the effects of trust, conflict, and collaboration on performance. *Project Management Journal, 42*(6), 78–91. doi: 10.1002/pmj.20268

Chiocchio, F., Grenier, S., O'Neill, T. A., Savaria, K., & Willms, D. J. (2012). The effects of collaboration on performance: A multilevel validation in project teams. *International Journal of Project Organisation and Management, 4*(1), 1–37. doi: 10.1504/IJPOM .2012.045362

Chiocchio, F., & Lafrenière, A. (2009). A project management perspective on student's declarative commitments to goals established within asynchronous communication. *Journal of Computer Assisted Learning, 25*(3), 294–305.

Chiocchio, F., Messikomer, C., Hobbs, B., Allen, N., & Lamerson, C. (2011, 14–16 April). *'Human factors' in project management research: Where is I/O psychology?* Paper presented at the 26th annual Society for Industrial and Organizational Psychology conference, Chicago, IL.

Choi, J. N., & Kim, M. U. (1999). The organizational application of groupthink and its limitations in organizations. *Journal of Applied Psychology, 84*(2), 297–306.

Cohen, J. (1988). *Statistical power analysis for the behavioral sciences* (2nd ed.). Hillsdale (NJ): Lawrence Erlbaum.

Cohen, J. (1992). A power primer. *Psychological Bulletin, 112*(1), 155–159.

Cohen, J. (1994). The earth is round ($p <$ .05). *American Psychologist, 49*(12), 997–1003.

Cohen, S., Kamarck, T., & Mermelstein, R. (1983). A global measure of perceived stress. *Journal of Health and Social Behavior, 24*, 386–396.

Cohen, S., & Wills, T. A. (1985). Stress, social support, and the buffering hypothesis. *Psychological Bulletin, 98*(2), 310–357.

Cohen, S. G., & Bailey, D. E. (1997). What makes teams work: Group effectiveness research from the shop floor to the executive suite. *Journal of Management, 23*(3), 239–290.

Connolly, J. J., & Viswesvaran, C. (2000). The role of affectivity in job satisfaction: A meta-analysis. *Personality and Individual Differences, 29*, 265–281.

Cooper, C. L., Dewe, P. J., & O'Driscoll, M. P. (Eds.). (2001). *Organizational Stress*. Thousand Oaks, CA: SAGE.

Crant, J. M. (2000). Proactive behavior in organizations. *Journal of Management, 26*, 435–462.

Cronbach, L. J. (1951). Coefficient Alpha and the internal structure of tests. *Psychomterika, 16*(3), 297–334.

Cunningham, L. L., & Dunn, V. B. (2001). Interprofessionnal policy analysis : An aid to public policy formation. *Theory into Practice, 26*, 129–133.

Curley, C., McEachern, J., & Speroff, T. (1998). A firm trial of interdisciplinaryrounds on the inpatient medical wards. *Medical Care, 36*, AS4–AS12.

Cutrona, C. E., & Russell, D. W. (1987). The provisions of social relationships and adaptation to stress. *Advances in Personal Relationships, 1*, 37–67.

D'Amour, D., Ferrada-Videla, M., San Martin Rodriguez, L., & Beaulieu, M.-D. (2005). The conceptual basis for interprofessional collaboration: Core concepts and theoretical frameworks. *Journal of Interprofessional Care, 19*(2), 116–131.

D'Amour, D., Goulet, L., Ladadie, J.-F., San Martin-Rodriguez, L., & Pineault, R. (2008). A model of typology of collaboration between professional healthcare organizations. *BMC Health Services Research, 8*, 188.

D'Amour, D., Sicotte, C., & Lévy, R. (1999). Un modèle de structuration de l'action collective au sein d'équipes interprofessionnelles dans les services de santé de première ligne. *Sciences sociales et santé, 17*(3), 67–94.

D'Souza, R. M., Strazdins, L., Lim, L., L-Y, Broom, D. H., & Rodgers, B. (2003). Work and health in a contemporary society: demands, control, and insecurity. *Journal of Epidemiology and Community Health, 57*, 849–854.

Danna, K., & Griffin, R. W. (1999). Health and well-being in the workplace: A review and synthesis of literature. *Journal of Management, 25*(3), 357–384.

Davezies, P. (2005). La santé au travail, une construction collective. *Santé et Travail, 52,* 24–28.

Davezies, P. (2010). Sur le rapport à l'autorité en clinique du travail. In F. Hubault (Ed.), *Pouvoir d'agir et autorité dans le travail* (pp. 31–40). Toulouse, France: Octares.

De Dreu, C. K. W., Evers, A., Beersma, B., Kluwer, E. S., & Nauta, A. (2001). A theory-based measure of conflict management strategies in the workplace. *Journal of Organizational Behavior, 22,* 645–668.

De Dreu, C. K. W., & Van Vianen, A. E. M. (2001). Managing relationship conflict and the effectiveness of organizational teams. *Journal of Organizational Behavior, 22,* 309–328.

De Dreu, C. K. W., & Weingart, L. R. (2003). Task versus relationship conflict, team performance, and team member satisfaction: A meta-analysis. *Journal of Applied Psychology, 88*(4), 741–749.

de Wit, F. R. C., Greer, L. L., & Jehn, K. A. (in press). The paradox of intragroup conflict: A meta-analysis. *Journal of Applied Psychology.*

Deci, E. L., Connell, J. P., & Ryan, R. M. (1989). Self-Determination in a Work Organization. *Journal of Applied Psychology, 74*(4), 580–590. doi: 10.1037/0021–9010.74.4.580

Dejours, C. (1980). Travail, usure mentale : essai de psychopathologie du travail. Paris: Le Centurion.

Dejours, C. (1994). *Le Facteur humain.* Paris: Presses universitaires de France.

Dejours, C. (2000). De la psychopathologie à la psychodynamique du travail (Travail, usure mentale : essai de psychopathologie du travail). Paris: Bayard.

Dejours, C. (2009a). Travail vivant 1 : Sexualité et travail. Paris: Payot.

Dejours, C. (2009b). Travail vivant 2 : travail et émancipation. Paris: Payot.

Diener, E., Gohm, C., Suh, E., & Oishi, S. (1998). Similarity of the relations between marital status and subjective well-being across cultures. *Journal of Cross-Cultural Psychology, 31*(4), 419–436.

Drinka, T. J., & Clark, P. G. (2000). *Health care teamwork : Interdisciplinary practice and teaching.* Westport, CT: Greenwood Publishing Goup, Inc.

Driskell, J. E., & Salas, E. (1991). Group decision making under stress. *Journal of Applied Psychology, 76,* 473–478.

Driskell, J. E., Salas, E., & Johnston, J. H. (1999). Does stress lead to a loss of team perspective? *Group Dynamics, 3,* 1–12.

Dutton, R. P., Cooper, C., Jones, A., Leone, S., Kramer, M. E., & Scalea, T. M. (2003). Daily multidisciplinary rounds shorten length of stay for trauma patients. *Journal of Trauma, 55,* 913–919.

Dwyer, J., Stanton, P., & Thiessen, V. (2004). *Project Management in Health and Community Services.* London: Routledge.

Edum-Fotwe, F. T., & McCaffer, R. (2000). Developing project management competency: Perspectives from the construction industry. *International Journal of Project Management, 18,* 111–124.

Edwards, J. R. (1994). Regression analysis as an alternative to difference scores. *Journal of Management, 20*(3), 683–689.

Edwards, J. R. (2001). Ten Difference Score Myths. *Organizational Research Methods, 4*(3), 265–287. doi: 10.1177/109442810143005

Edwards, J. R., Cable, D. M., Williamson, I. O., Lambert, L. S., & Shipp, A. J. (2006). The phenomenology of fit: Linking the person and environment to the subjective experience of person-environment fit. *Journal of Applied Psychology, 91*(4), 802–827. doi: 10.1037/0021-9010.91.4.802

Edwards, J. R., & Parry, M. E. (1993). On the Use of Polynomial Regression Equations as an Alternative to Difference Scores in Organizational Research. *The Academy of Management Journal, 36*(6), 1577–1613.

Ellis, A. P. J. (2006). System breakdown: The role of mental models and transactive memory in the relationship between acute stress and team performance. *Academy of Management Journal, 49*(6), 576–589.

Elovainio, M., & Kivimäki, M. (1996). Occupational stresses, goal clarity, control, and strain among nurses in the finnish health care system. *Research in Nursing & Health, 19*(6), 517–524. doi: 10.1002/(sici)1098–240x(199612)19:6<517::aid-nur7>3.0.co;2–r

Farrell, M. P., Schmitt, M. H., & Heinemann, G. D. (2001). Informal roles and the stages of interdisciplinary team development. *Journal of Interprofessional Care, 15*(3), 281–295. doi: doi:10.1080/13561820120068980

Fleury, M.-J., Grenier, G., Cazal, L., & Perrault, M. (2008). Integration strategies in mental health care: Lessons Drawn from a pilot project. *Canadian Journal of Community Mental Health, 27*(1), 111–124.

Fleury, M.-J., Tremblay, M., Nguyen, H., & Bordeleau, L. (Eds.). (2007). *Le système socio-sanitaire au Québec*. Montréal, Qc, Canada: Gaëtan Morin Editeur.

Foushee, H. C., & Helmreich, R. L. (1988). Group interaction and flight crew performance. In E. L. Wiener & D. C. Nagel (Eds.), *Human Factors in Aviation*. San Diego, CA: Academic Press.

Frank, J. R. (Ed.). (2005). *The CanMEDS 2005 Physician Competency Framework*. Ottawa, Canada: The Royal College of Physicians and Surgeons of Canada.

Friedman, R. A., Tidd, S. T., Currall, S. C., & Tsai, J. C. (2000). What Goes Around Comes Around: the Impact of Personal Conflict Style on Work Conflict and Stress. *The International Journal of Conflict Management, 11*(1), 32–55.

Gagné, M., & Deci, E. L. (2005). Self-Determination theory and work motivation. *Journal of Organizational Behavior, 26*, 331–362.

Gällstedt, M. (2003). Working conditions in projects: Perceptions of stress and motivation among project team members and project managers. *International Journal of Project Management, 21*, 449–455.

Ganster, D. C. (2008). Measurement challenges for studying work-related stressors and strains. *Human Resource Management Review, 18*, 259–270.

Gareis, R., & Huemann, M. (2007). Maturity models for the project-oriented company. In R. Turner (Ed.), *Gower Handbook of Project Management* (4th ed., pp. 183–208). Surrey, England: Gower.

Garland, D. J., & Barry, J. R. (1990). Personality and leader behaviors in collegiate football: A multidimensional approach to performance. *Journal of Research in Personality, 24*(3), 355–370.

Garman, A. N., Corrigan, P. W., & Morris, S. (2002). Staff burnout and patient satisfaction: Evidence of relationships at the care unit level. *Journal of Occupational Health Psychology*, 7(3), 235–241.

Gelbard, R., & Carmeli, A. (2009). The interactive effect of team dynamics and organizational support in ICT project sucess. *International Journal of Project Management*, 27, 464–470.

Gevers, J., Van Erven, P., De Jonge, J., Maas, M., & De Jong, J. (2010). Effect of acute and chronic job demands on effective individual teamwork behaviour in medical emergencies. *Journal of Advanced Nursing*, 66(7), 1573–1583.

Goetzel, R. Z., Long, S. R., Ozminkowski, R. J., Hawkins, K., Wang, S., & Lynch, W. (2004). Health, Absence, Disability, and Presenteeism Cost Estimates of Certain Physical and Mental Health Conditions Affecting U.S. Employers. *Journal of Occupational and Environmental Medicine*, 46(4), 398–412.

Goldebhar, L. M., LaMontagne, A. D., Katz, T., Heaney, C., & Landsbergis, P. (2001). The Intervention research process in occupational safety and health: An Overview from the national occupational research agenda intervention effectiveness research team. *Journal of Occupational Environment Medicine*, 43, 616–622.

Goldman, J., Meuser, J., Lawrie, L., Rogers, J., & Reeves, S. (2010). Interprofessional primary care protocols: A strategy to promote an evidence-based approach to teamwork and the delivery of care. *Journal of Interprofessional Care*, 24(6), 663–665.

Goldman, J., Meuser, J., Rogers, J., & Reeves, S. (2010). Interprofessional collaboration in family health teams: An Ontario-based study. . *Canadian Family Physician*, 56, 368–374.

Goodman, P. S. (1986). Impact of task and technology on group performance. In P. S. E. Goodman (Ed.), *Designing effective work groups*. San Francisco: Jossey-Bass.

Grieshaber, L. D. (Ed.). (1997). *The Healthcare Practitioner's Handbook of Management*. Boca Raton, FL: St. Lucie Press.

Griffin, M. A., Neal, A., & Parker, S. K. (2007). A new model of work role performance: Positive behavior in uncertain and interdependent contexts. *Academy of Management Journal*, 50(2), 327–347.

Gully, S. M., Devine, D. J., & Whitney, D. J. (1995). A meta-analysis of cohesion and performance: Effects of levels of analysis and task interdependence. *Small Group Research*, 26(4), 497–520.

Gully, S. M., Incalcaterra, K. A., Joshi, A., & Beaubien, J. M. (2002). A meta-analysis of team-efficacy, potency, and performance: Interdependence and level of analysis as moderators of observed relationships. *Journal of Applied Psychology*, 87(5), 819–832.

Gundlach, M., Zivnuska, S., & Stoner, J. (2006). Understanding the relationship between individualismcollectivism and team performance through an integration of social identity theory and the social relations model. *Human Relations*, 59, 1603–1632.

Guzzo, R. A., & Shea, G. P. (1992). Group performance and intergroup relations in organizations. In M. D. Dunnette, Hough, L.M. (Ed.), *Handbook of Industrial and Organizational Psychology* (Vol. 2nd ed., pp. 269–313). Palo Alto: Consulting psychologists Press.

Guzzo, R. A., Yost, P. R., Campbell, R. J., & Shea, G. P. (1993). Potency in groups: Articulating a construct. *British Journal of Social Psychology, 32*, 87–106.

Hackman, R. J. (1987). The design of work teams. In J. W. Lorsch (Ed.), *Handbook of Organizational Behavior* (pp. 315–342). Englewood Cliffs, NJ: Prentice-Hall.

Hackman, R. J. (Ed.). (1990). Groups That Work (And Those That Don't): Creating Conditions For Effective Teamwork. San Francisco, CA: Jossey-Bass.

Harmon, S. K., Brallier, S. A., & Brown, G. F. (2002). Organizational and team context. In G. D. Heinemann & A. M. Zeiss (Eds.), *Team Performance in Health Care* (pp. 57–70). New York: Kluwer Academic/Plenum Publishers.

Häusser, A. J., Mojzisch, A., Niesel, M., & Schulz-Hardt, S. (2010). Ten years on: A review of recent research on the Job Demand-Control (-Support) model and psychological well-being. *Work and Stress, 24*(1), 1–35.

Headrick, L. A., Wilcock, P. M., & Batalden, P. B. (1998). Interprofessional working and continuing medical education. *BMJ, 316*(7133), 771–774.

Heinemann, G. D. (2002). Teams in health care settings. In G. D. Heinemann & A. M. Zeiss (Eds.), *Team Performance in Health Care* (pp. 3–17). New York: Kluwer Academic/Plenum Publishers.

Henriksen, K., & Dayton, E. (2006). Organizational silence and hidden threats to patient safety. *Health Service Ressearch, 41*(4), 1539–1554. doi: 10.1111/j.1475–6773.2006.00564.x

Herbert, C. P. (2005). Changing the culture: Interprofessional education for collaborative patient-centred practice in Canada. *Journal of Interprofessional Care, 19*(s1), 1–4. doi:10.1080/13561820500081539

Hoegl, M., Weinkauf, K., & Gemuenden, H. G. (2004). Interteam coordination, project commitment, and teamwork in multiteam R&D projects: A longitudinal study. *Organization Science, 15*(1), 38–55.

Hurtz, G. H., & Donovan, J. L. (2000). Personality and Job Performance: The Big Five revisited. *Journal of Applied Psychology, 85*(6), 869–879.

Ibbs, C. W., Reginato, J. M., & Hoon Kwak, Y. (2007). Developing project management capability: Benchmarking, maturity, modeling, gap analysis, and ROI studies. In P. W. G. Morris & J. K. Pinto (Eds.), *The Wiley Guide to Project Organization & Project Management Competencies* (pp. 270–289). Hoboken, NJ: Wiley.

Institut de psychodynamique du travail du Québec. (2006). Espace de réflexion, espace d'action en santé mentale au travail - Enquêtes en psychodynamique du travail au Québec. Québec, Canada: Les Presses de l'Université Laval.

Ivancevich, J., & Matteson, M. (1980). Stress at Work: A managerial perspective. In J. C. Quick, R. S. Bhagat, J. E. Dalton & J. D. Quick (Eds.), *Work stress: Health care systems in the workplace*. New York: Praeger.

Jacobsson, C., Pousette, A., & Thylefors, I. (2001). Managing Stress and Feelings of Mastery among Swedish Comprehensive School Teachers. *Scandinavian Journal of Educational Research, 45*(1), 37–53. doi: 10.1080/00313830020023384

Jehn, K. A. (1995). A multimethod examination of the benefits and detriments of intragroup conflict. *Administrative Science Quarterly, 40*(2), 256–282.

Jehn, K. A., & Bendersky, C. (2003). Intragroup conflict in organizations: A contingency perspective on the conflict-outcome relationship. *Research in Organizational Behavior, 25*, 187–242.

Jehn, K. A., Bezrukova, K., & Thatcher, S. (2008). Conflict, diversity, and faultlines in workgroups. In C. K. W. De Dreu & M. J. Gelfand (Eds.), *The Psychology of Conflict Management in Organizations* (pp. 179–210). New York: Laurence Erlbaum.

Jehn, K. A., & Mannix, E. (2001). The dynamic nature of conflict: A longitudinal study of intra-group conflict and group performance. *Academy of Management Journal, 42*(2), 238–251.

Jex, S. M. (Ed.). (1998). *Stress and Job Performance*. Thousands Oaks, CA: Sage.

Jex, S. M., Adams, G. A., Bachrach, D. G., & Sorenson, S. (2003). The impact of situational constraints, role stressors, and commitment on employee altruism. *Journal of Occupational Health Psychology, 8*(3), 171–180.

Jex, S. M., & Thomas, J. L. (2003). Relations between stressors and group perceptions: Main and mediating effects. *Work & Stress, 17*(2), 158–169.

Kahneman, D., Diener, E., & Schwarz, N. (1999). *Well-being: The foundations of hedonic psychology*. New York: Russell Sage Foundation.

Kanfer, R., Chen, G., & Pritchard, R. D. (Eds.). (2008). *Work Motivation: Past, Present, and Future*. New York: Routledge.

Kanter, R. M. (1986). Empowering people to act on ideas. *Executive Excellence, February*, 5–6.

Karasek, R. (1979). Job demands, job decision latitude and mental strain: Implications for job re-design. *Administrative Science Quarterly, 24*, 285–309.

Karasek, R., & Theorell, T. (1990). Healthy Work: Stress, productivity, and the reconstruction of working life. La Vergne, TN: Basic Books.

Katz, D., & Kahn, R. L. (1978). *The Social Psychology of Organizations* (2nd ed.). New York: Wiley.

Keegan, A., Turner, R., & Huemann, M. (2007). Managing human resources in the project-based organization. In R. Turner (Ed.), *Gower Handbook of Project Management* (4th ed., pp. 649–676). Surrey, England: Gower.

Kenny, N. P., Mann, K. V., & MacLeod, H. (2003). Role Modeling in Physicians' Professional Formation: Reconsidering an Essential but Untapped Educational Strategy. *Academic Medicine, 78*(12), 1203–1210.

Kerzner, H. (2003). Project Management: A Systems Approach to Planning, Scheduling, and Controlling. (8th ed.). Hoboken, NJ: John Wiley & Sons.

Kerzner, H. (Ed.). (1998). In Search of Excellence in Project Management: Successful Practices in High Performance Organizations. New York: Van Nostrand Reinhold.

Keyes, C. L. M., & Lopez, S. J. (2002). Toward a science of mental health: Positive directions in diagnosis and interventions. In C. R. Snyder & S. J. Lopez (Eds.), *Handbook of positive psychology* (pp. 45–59). New York: Oxford University Press.

Kiggundu, M. N. (1983). Task interdependence and job design: Test of a theory. *Organizational Behavior & Human Performance, 31*(2), 145–172.

Kingdon, D. G. (1992). Interprofessional collaboration in mental health. *Journal of Inter-professional Care, 6*(2), 141–147.

Kirkpatrick, D. (1996). Great ideas revisited. Techniques for evaluating training programs. Revisiting Kirkpatrick's fourlevel model. *Training and Development, 50*(1), 54–59.

Klein, J. T. (2012). A Taxonomy of Interdisciplinarity. In R. Frodeman, J. T. Klein & C. Mitcham (Eds.), *The Oxford Handbook of Interdisciplinarity*. Oxford, UK: Oxford University Press.

Kolb, D. A. (1984). Experiential Learning: Experience as the Source of LEarning and Development. Englewood Cliffs, NJ: Prentice-Hall.

Kozlowski, S. W. J., & Bell, B. S. (2003). Work groups and teams in organizations. In W. C. Borman, D. R. Ilgen, R. Klimoski, J. & I. B. Weiner (Eds.), *Handbook of Psychology: Industrial and Organizational Psychology* (Vol. 12, pp. 333–375). London: Wiley.

Kozlowski, S. W. J., Gully, S. M., Nason, E. R., & Smith, E. M. (1999). Developing adaptive teams: A Theory of compilation and performance accross levels and time. In E. D. Pulakos & D. R. Ilgen (Eds.), *The Changing Nature of Performance* (pp. 240–292). San Francisco: Jossey-Bass.

Kozlowski, S. W. J., & Ilgen, D. R. (2006). Enhancing the effectiveness of work groups and teams. *Psychological Science in the Public Interest, 7*(3), 77–124.

Krause, N. (1995). Assessing stress-buffering effects: A cautionary note. *Psychology and Aging, 10*(4), 518–526.

Kubovy, M. (1999). On the pleasures of the mind. In D. Kahneman, D. E. Diener & N. Schwartz (Eds.), *Well-Being: The Foundations of Hedonic Psychology* (pp. 134–154). New York: Russell Sage Foundation.

Lam, P. K., & Chin, K. S. (2004). Project factors influencing conflict intensity and handling styles in collaborative NPD. *Creativity and Innovation Management, 3*(March), 52–62.

Lance, C. E., Butts, M. M., & Michels, L., C. (2006). The Sources of Four Commonly Reported Cutoff Criteria: What Did They Really Say? *Organizational Research Methods, 9*(2), 202–220.

Lee, K., & Allen, J. (2002). Organizational citizenship behavior and work place deviance: The role of affect and cognitions. *Journal of Applied Social Psychology, 87*, 131–142.

Locke, E. A., & Latham, G. P. (2002). Building a Practically Useful Theory of Goal Setting and Task Motivation. *American Psychologist, 57*(9), 705–717.

Locke, E. A., & Latham, G. P. (Eds.). (1990). *A theory of goal setting and task performance.* Englewood Cliffs, NJ: Prentice Hall.

Lowe, F., & O'Hara, S. (2000). Multi-disciplinary team working in practice: managing the transition. *Journal of Interprofessional Care, 14*(3), 269–279.

Lyubomirsky, S., King, L., & Diener, E. (2005). The benefits of frequent positive affect: Does happiness lead to success? *Psychological Bulletin, 131*, 803–855.

Manning, F. J., & Fullerton, T. D. (1988). Health and Well-Being in Highly Cohesive Units of the U.S. Army. *Journal of Applied Social Psychology, 18*(6), 503–519. doi: 10.1111/j.1559-1816.1988.tb00032.x

Manser, T. (2009). Teamwork and patient safety in dynamic domains of healthcare: A review of the litterature. *Acta Anaesthesiol Scand, 53*, 143–151.

Marks, M. A., Mathieu, J. E., & Zaccaro, S. J. (2001). A Temporally based framework and taxonomy of team processes. *Academy of Management Review, 26*(3), 356–376.

Maslow, A. H. (1943). A theory of human motivation. *Psychological Review, 50*(4), 370–396.

Massé, R., Poulin, C., Dassa, C., Lambert, J., Bélair, S., & Battaglini, A. (1998a). Élaboration et validation d'un outil de mesure de la détresse psychologique au Québec [Development and validation of a measure of psychological distress in Quebec]. *Revue Canadienne de Santé Publique, 89*, 183–189.

Massé, R., Poulin, C., Dassa, C., Lambert, J., Bélair, S., & Battaglini, A. (1998b). Élaboration et validation d'un outil de mesure du bien-être psychologique au Québec [Development and validation of a measure of psychological well-being in Quebec]. *Revue Canadienne de Santé Publique, 89,* 352–357.

Mathews, K. E., & Canon, L. K. (1975). Environmental noise level as a determinant of helping behavior. *Journal of Personality and Social Psychology, 32,* 517–577.

Mathieu, J. E., Heffner, T. S., Goodwin, G. F., Salas, E., & Cannon-Bowers, J. A. (2000). The influence of shared mental models on team process and performance. *Journal of Applied Psychology, 85*(2), 273–283.

McDaid, D. (2008). *Mental Health in Workplace Settings. Consensus paper.* Luxembourg: European Communities.

McIntyre, R. M., & Salas, E. (1995). Measuring and managing for team performance: Emerging principles from complex environments. In R. A. Guzzo & E. Salas (Eds.), *Team effectivness and decision making in organizations* (pp. 9–45). San Francisco: Jossey Bass.

McVicar, A. (2003). Workplace stress in nursing: a literature review. *Journal of Advanced Nursing, 44,* 633–642.

Mintzberg, H. (1979). *The structuring of organizations.* Englewood Cliffs, NJ: Prentice-Hall.

Mintzberg, H. (1982). Structure et dynamique des organisations [The Structuring of Organizations]. Paris: Éditions d'Organisation.

Mitchell, R., Parker, V., Giles, M., & White, N. (2010). Review: Toward Realizing the Potential of Diversity in Composition of Interprofessional Health Care Teams. *Medical Care Research and Review, 67*(1), 3–26. doi: 10.1177/1077558709338478

Molinier, P. (2006). Les enjeux psychiques du travail. Introduction à la psychodynamique du travail. . Paris, France: Petite Bibliothèque Payot.

Motowidlo, S. J. (2003). Job Performance. In W. C. Borman, D. R. Ilgen, R. Klimoski, J. & I. B. Weiner (Eds.), *Handbook of Psychology : Industrial and Organizational Psychology* (Vol. 12, pp. 39–53). London: Wiley.

Nordqvist, S., Hovmark, S., & Zika-Viktorsson, A. (2004). Perceived time pressure and social processes in project teams. *International Journal of Project Management, 22*(6), 463–468.

Nunnally, J. C., & Bernstein, I. H. (1994). *Psychometric Theory* (3rd ed.). New York: McGraw-Hill.

O'Leary, K. J., Buck, R., Fligiel, H. M., Haviley, C., Slade, M. E., Landler, M. P., . . . Wayne, D. B. (2011). Structured interdisciplinary rounds in a medical teaching unit: Improving patient safety. *Archives of Internal Medicine, 171*(7), 678–684.

Orchard, C. (2008, November 17). [Presentation on patient-centered care to CASN Nurse Educators Conference].

Parker, S. K., Williams, H., M., & Turner, N. (2006). Modeling the antecedents of proactive behavior at work. *Journal of Applied Psychology, 91,* 636–652. doi: 10.1037/0021-9010.91.3.636

Pearson, K. (1896). Mathematical Contributions to the Theory of Evolution. III. Regression, Heredity and Panmixia. *Philosophical Transactions of the Royal Society of London. Series A, 187,* 253–318.

Pelled, L. H., & Xin, K. R. (1999). Down and out: An investigation of the relationship between mood and employee withdrawal behavior. *Journal of Management*, *25*(6), 875–895.

Pellegrinelli, S., & Murray-Webster, R. (2011). Multi-paradigmatic perspectives on a business transformation program. *Project Management Journal*, *42*(6), 4–19. doi: 10.1002/pmj.20275

Peterson, U., Demerouti, E., Bergström, G., Asberg, M., & Nygren, A. (2008). Work characteristics and sickness absence in burnout and nonburnout groups: A study of Swedish health care workers. *International Journal of Stress Management*, *15*(2), 153–172.

Pich, M. T., Loch, C. H., & Meyer, A. D. (2002). On Uncertainty, Ambiguity, and Complexity in Project Management. *Management Science*, *48*(8), 1008–1023. doi: 10.1287/mnsc.48.8.1008.163

Pierce, G. R., Sarason, B. R., Sarason, I. G., Joseph, H. J., & Henderson, C. A. (1996). Conceptualizing and assessing social support in the context of the family. In G. R. Pierce, B. R. Sarason & I. G. Sarason (Eds.), *Handbook of social support and the family* (pp. 3–23). New York: Plenum Press.

Pondy, L. R. (1967). Organizational conflict: Concepts and models. *Administrative Science Quarterly*, *12*, 296–320.

Programme de lutte contre le cancer. (1997). *Pour lutter efficacement contre le cancer, formons équipe*. (Publication no : 97–729–50F). Gouvernement du Québec, Bibliothèque nationale du Québec.

Project Management Institute. (2003). *Organizational project management maturity model (OPM3): Knowledge foundation*. Newtown Square, PA: Project Management Institute.

Project Management Institute. (2008). *A Guide to the Project Management Body of Knowledge (PMBOK® Guide)* (4th ed.). Newtown Square, PA: Project Management Institute.

Project Management Institute (Ed.). (2002). *Project manager competency development framework*. Newtown Square, PA: Project Management Institute.

Pruitt, D. G., & Rubin, J. (1986). *Social Conflict: Excalation, Stalemate and Settlment*. New York: Random House.

Raudenbush, S. W., & Bryk, A. S. (Eds.). (2002). *Hierarchical Linear Models* (2nd ed.). Thousand Oaks, CA: Sage.

Reeves, S., Zwarenstein, M., Goldman, J., Barr, H., Freeth, D., Koppel, I., & Hammick, M. (2010). The effectiveness of interprofessional education: Key findings from a new systematic review. *Journal of Interprofessional Care*, *24*(3), 230–241.

Rhoades, L., & Eisenberger, R. (2002). Perceived Organizational Support: A Review of the Literature. *Journal of Applied Psychology*, *87*(4), 698–714. doi: 10.1037/0021-9010.87.4.698

Rich, M. W., Beckham, V., Wittenberh, C., Levens, C. L., Freedland, K. E., & Carney, R. M. (1995). A multidisciplinary intervention to prevent the readmission of elderly patients with congestive heart failure. *New England Journal of Medicine*, *333*, 1190–1195.

Rivard, P. (2006). La gestion de la formation en entreprise : Pour préserver et accroître le capital compétence de votre organisation. Québec, Canada: Presses de l'Université du Québec.

Rosenfeld, L. B., & Richman, J. M. (1997). Developing effective social support: Team building and the social support process. *Journal of Applied Sport Psychology, 9*(1), 133–153.

Rosenthal, R., & Rubin, D. B. (1982). A simple, general purpose display of magnitude of experimental effect. *Journal of Educational Psychology, 74*(2), 166–169.

Ryan, R. M., & Deci, E. L. (2001). To be happy or to be self-fulfilled: A review of research on hedonic and eudaimonic well-being. In S. E. Fiske (Ed.), *Annual Review of Psychology* (Vol. 52, pp. 141–166). Palo Alto, CA: Annual Reviews.

Ryff, C. D. (1995). Psychological well-being in adult life. *Current Directions in Psychological Scien, 4*, 99–104.

Ryff, C. D., & Keyes, C. L. (1995). The Structure of Psychological Well-Being Revisited. *Journal of Personal Social Psychology, 69*(4), 719–729.

Saks, A. M., & Haccoun, R. R. (2010). *Managing performance through training and development* (5th ed.). Toronto, Canada: Nelson Education Ltd.

Salas, E., & Fiore, S. M. (Eds.). (2004). *Team cognition: Understanding the factors that drive process and performance.* Washington (DC): American Psychological Association.

Salas, E., Priest, H. A., Stagl, K. C., Sims, D., & Burke, S. (2007). Work teams in organizations: A historical reflection and lessons learned. In L. L. Koppes (Ed.), *Historical Perspectives in Industrial and Organizational Psychology* (pp. 407–438). Mahwah, NJ: Erlbaum.

Sanne, B., Mykletun, A., Dahl, A. A., Moen, B. E., & Tell, G. S. (2005). Testing the Job Demand–Control–Support model with anxiety and depression as outcomes: The Hordaland Health Study. *Occupational Medicine, 55*(6), 463–473. doi: 10.1093/occmed/kqi071

Sawyer, J. E. (1992). Goal and process clarity: Specification of multiple constructs of role ambiguity and a structural equation model of their antecedents and consequences. *Journal of Applied Psychology, 77*(2), 130–142.

Schliesman, E. S. (1987). Relationship between the congruence of preferred and actual leader behavior and subordinate satisfaction with leadership. *Journal of Sport Behavior, 10*(3), 157–166.

Schmitt, M., Blue, A., Aschenbrener, C. A., & Viggiano, T. R. (2011). Core Competencies for Interprofessional Collaborative Practice: Reforming Health Care by Transforming Health Professionals' Education. *Academic Medicine, 86*(11), 1351 1310.1097/ACM.1350b1013e3182308e3182339.

Scholes, J., & Vaughan, B. (2002). Crossboundary working: implications for the multi-professional team. *Journal of Clinical Nursing, 11*, 399–408.

Schön, D. A. (1983). *The Reflective Practitioner.* USA: Basic Books.

Schwenk, C., & Valacich, J. S. (1994). Effects of Devil's Advocacy and Dialectical Inquiry on Individuals versus Groups. *Organizational Behavior and Human Decision Processes, 59*(2), 210–222. doi: 10.1006/obhd.1994.1057

Segal, B. S. (1994). Developing the interprofessional team. In G. J. Agich (Ed.), *The clinical care of aged persons : An interdisciplinary perspective.* New Yord: Oxford University Press.

Shea, G. P., & Guzzo, R. A. (1987). Groups as human resources. In K. M. Rowland & G. R. Ferris (Eds.), *Research in human resources and personnel management* (Vol. 5, pp. 323–356). Greenwich, CT: JAI Press.

Sicotte, C., D'Amour, D., & Moreault, M.-P. (2002). Interdisciplinary collaboration within Quebec community health care centres. *Social Science & Medicine, 55*(6), 991–1003.

Siegrist, J. (1996). Adverse health effects of high-effort/low-reward conditions. *Journal of Occupational Health Psychology, 1*(1), 27–41. doi: 10.1037/1076–8998.1.1.27

Simons, T. L., & Peterson, R. S. (2000). Task conflict and relationship conflict in top management teams: The pivotal role of intragroup trust. *Journal of Applied Psychology, 85*(1), 102–111.

Software Engineering Institute. (2005). *Capability Maturity Model Integration (CMMI) Overview*. Pittsburgh, PA: Carnegie Mellon University.

Software Engineering Institute. (2006). *CMMI for development, Version 1.2*. Pitsburgh, PA: Carnegie Mellon University.

Souba, W., Way, D., Lucey, C., Sedmak, D., & Notestine, M. (2011). Elephants in Academic Medicine. *Academic Medicine, 86*(12), 1492–1499 1410.1097/ ACM.1490b1013e3182356559.

Spreitzer, G. M. (1996). Social Structural Characteristics of Psychological Empowerment. *Academy of Management Journal, 39*(2), 483–504.

Stewart, W. F., Ricci, J. A., Chee, E., Hahn, S. R., & Morganstein, D. (2003). Cost of Lost Productive Work Time Among US Workers With Depression. *JAMA: The Journal of the American Medical Association, 289*(23), 3135–3144. doi: 10.1001/jama.289.23.3135

Strasser, D. C., Falconer, J. A., Herrin, J., Bowen, S. E., Stevens, A. B., & Uomoto, J. M. (2005). Team functioning and patient outcomes in stroke rehabilitation. *Arch Phys Med Rehabil, 86*, 403–409.

Stratman, J. K., & Roth, A. V. (2002). Enterprise Resource Planning (ERP) Competence Constructs: Ibo-Stage Multi-Item Scale Development and Validation. *Decision Sciences, 33*(4), 601–628.

Strazdins, L., D'Souza, R. M., Lim, L., L-Y, Broom, D. H., & Rodgers, B. (2004). Job strain, job insecurity, and health: Rethinking the relationship. *Journal of Occupational Health Psychology, 9*(4), 296–305.

Stretton, A. M. (2006). Bodies of knowledge and competency standards in project management. In P. C. Dinsmore & J. Cabanis-Brewin (Eds.), *The AMA Handbook of Project Management* (pp. 15–24). New York: Amacom American Management Association.

Stride, C., Wall, T. D., & Catley, N. (Eds.). (2007). Measures of job satisfaction, organisational commitment, mental health and job related well-being - A benchmarking manual (2nd ed.). West Sussex, England: Wiley.

Sundstrom, E., McIntyre, M., Halfhill, T., & Richards, H. (2000). Work groups: From the Hawthorne studies to work teams of the 1990s and beyond. *Group Dynamics, 4*(1), 44–67. doi: 10.1037/1089–2699.4.1.44

Tabachnick, B. G., & Fidell, L. S. (2007). *Using multivariate statistics* (5th ed.). Boston: Pearson.

Tesluk, P., Mathieu, J. E., Zaccaro, S. J., & Marks, M. (1997). Task and aggregation issues in the analysis and assessment of team performance. In M. T. Brannick, E. Salas & C. Prince (Eds.), *Team Performance Assessment and Measurement* (pp. 197–224). Mahwah (NJ): Lawrence Erlbaum.

Therriault, P.-Y. (2010). Changements organisationnel et technologique, santé mentale et travail : Retour sur une enquête en psychodynamique du travail menée auprès de machinistes. Sarrebruck, Germany: Éditions universitaires européennes.

Therriault, P.-Y., Rhéaume, J., & Streit, U. (2004). Identité de métier en péril chez des machinistes suite à des transformations organisationnelles et technologiques. *Le Travail Humain, 67*(4), 333–357.

Thoresen, C. J., Kaplan, S. A., Barsky, A. P., Warren, C. R., & de Chermont, K. (2003). The affective underpinnings of job perceptions and attitudes: a meta-analytic review and integration. *Psychological Bulletin, 129,* 914–945.

Tjosvold, D. (2008). Conflicts in the study of conflicts in organizations. In C. K. W. De Dreu & M. J. Gelfand (Eds.), *The Psychology of Conflict Management in Organizations* (pp. 445–453). New York: Laurence Erlbaum.

Trudel, L. (1999). Évaluation interdisciplinaire d'un programme de formation à visées préventives dispensé à des travailleurs avec ordinateur - Analyse ergonomique et psychodynamique du travail. Unpublished Ph.D. dissertation, Université de Montréal, Montréal, Canada.

Tucker, A., & Edmondson, A. C. (2003). Why Hospitals Don't Learn from Failures: Organizational and Psychological Dynamics That Inhibit System Change. *California Management Review, 45,* 55–72.

Tuckman, B. W. (1965). Developmental sequence in small groups. *Psychological Bulletin, 63,* 384–399.

Tuckman, B. W., & Jensen, M., A., C. (1977). Stages in small group development revisited. *Group and Organizational Studies, 5,* 419–427.

Turner, R. (2009). *The Handbook of Project-Based Management* (3rd ed.). New York: McGraw-Hill.

Turner, R., & Müller, R. (2003). On the nature of the project as a temporary organization. *International Journal of Project Management, 21,* 1–8.

Uchida, S., Sznelwar, L. I., & Lancman, S. (2011). Aspects épistémologiques et méthodologiques de la psychodynamique du travail. *Travailler, 25,* 29–44.

Vagg, P. R., & Spielberger, C. D. (1998). Occupational stress: Measuring job pressure and organizational support in the workplace. *Journal of Occupational Health Psychology, 3*(4), 294–305. doi: 10.1037/1076–8998.3.4.294

Vahey, D. C., Aiken, L. H., Sloane, D. M., Clarke, S. P., & Vargas, D. (2004). Nurse Burnout and Patient Satisfaction. *Medical Care, 42*(2), 57–66.

Van de Vliert, E. (1997). Complex interpersonal conflict behaviour: Theoretical frontiers. Hove, England.: Psychology Press.

Van Der Doef, M., Maes, S., & Diekstra, R. (1999). An examination of the job demand-control-support model with various occupational strain indicators. *Anxiety, Stress, and Coping, 13*(2), 87–114.

Van Der Doef, M., Maes, S., & Diekstra, R. (2000). An examination of the job demand-control-support model with various occupational strain indicators. *Anxiety, Stress, and Coping, 13*(2), 165–185.

Van der Vegt, G., S., Van de Vliert, E., & Oosterhof, A. (2003). Informational dissimilarity and organizational citizenship behavior: The role of intrateam interdependence and team identification. *Academy of Management Journal, 46*(6), 715–727.

Van Katwyk, P. T., Fox, S., Spector, P. E., & Kelloway, E. K. (2000). Using the Job-related Affective Well-being Scale (JAWS) to investigate affective responses to work stressors. *Journal of Occupational Health Psychology, 5,* 219–230.

Vézina, M. (2000). Les fondements théoriques de la psychodynamique du travail In M.-C. C.-R. M. Vézina (Ed.), *Le travail et ses malentendus - Enquêtes en psychodynamique du travail au Québec* (pp. 29–42). Québec, Canada: Les Presses de l'Université Laval.

Vinokur-Kaplan, D. (1995). Treatment teams that work (and those that don't): An application of Hackman's Group Effectivness Model to interdisciplinary teams in psychiatric hospitals. *Journal of Applied Behavioral Science, 31*(3), 303–327.

Walsh, J. M., Harrison, J. D., Young, J. M., Butow, P. N., Solomon, M. J., & Masya, L. (2010). What are the current barriers to effective cancer care coordination? A qualitative study. *BMC Health Services Research 10,* 132.

Warr, P. (2005). Work, well-being, and mental health. In J. Barling, E. K. Kelloway & M. R. Frone (Eds.), *Handbook of Work Stress* (pp. 547–573). Thoudans Oaks, CA: Sage.

Waterman, A. S. (1993). Two conceptions of happiness: Contrasts of personal expressiveness (eudaimonia) and hedonic enjoyment. *Journal of Personality and Social Psychology, 64,* 678–691.

Way, D., Jones, L., & Busing, N. (2000). Implementation Strategies: "Collaboration in Primary Care – Family Doctors & Nurse Practitioners Delivering Shared Care". Toronto, Canada: The Ontario College of Family Physicians.

Wegner, D. M. (1986). Transactive memory: A contemporary analysis of the group mind. In B. Mullen & G. R. Goethals (Eds.), *Theories of group behavior.* New York: Springer-Verlag.

Weiss, M. R., & Friedrichs, W. D. (1986). The influence of leader behaviors, coach attributes, and institutional variables on performance and satisfaction of collegiate basketball teams. *Journal of Sport Psychology, 8*(332–346).

Weissmann, P. F., Branch, W. T., Gracey, C. F., Haidet, P., & Frankel, R. M. (2006). Role Modeling Humanistic Behavior: Learning Bedside Manner from the Experts. *Academic Medicine, 81*(7), 661–667.

Weldon, E., Jehn, K. A., & Pradhan, P. (1991). Processes that mediate the relationship between a group goal and improved group performance. *Journal of Personality and Social Psychology, 61*(4), 555–569.

Westre, K. R., & Weiss, M. R. (1991). The relationship between perceived coaching behaviors and group cohesion in high school football teams. *The Sport Psychologist, 5*(1), 41–54.

WHO World Mental Health Survey Consortium. (2004). Prevalence, Severity, and Unmet Need for Treatment of Mental Disorders in the World Health Organization World Mental Health Surveys. *JAMA: The Journal of the American Medical Association, 291*(21), 2581–2590. doi: 10.1001/jama.291.21.2581

Wilemon, D. (2002). Project management research: Experiences and perspectives. In D. P. Slevine, D. I. Cleland & J. K. Pinto (Eds.), *The Frontiers of Project Management Research* (pp. 57–71). Newtown Square, PA: Project Management Institute.

Williams, H. M., & Allen, N. J. (2008). Teams at work. In J. Barling & C. L. Cooper (Eds.), *The SAGE Handbook of Organizational Behavior—Volume 1—Micro Approaches* (pp. 141–159). Los Angeles, CA: SAGE.

Wong, C. S., & Campion, M. A. (1991). Development and test of a task level model of motivational job design. *Journal of Applied Psychology, 76,* 825–837.

Wong, S.-S., DeSanctis, G., & Staudenmayer, N. (2007). The Relationship Between Task Interdependency and Role Stress: A Revisit of the Job Demands–Control Model. *Journal of Management Studies, 44*(2), 284–303. doi: 10.1111/j.1467–6486.2007.00689.x

World Health Organization. (1946). Constitution of the World Health Organization. Retrieved December 12, 2011, from http://apps.who.int/gb/bd/PDF/bd47/EN/constitution-en.pdf

World Health Organization. (1985). Health manpower requirements for the achievement of health for all by the year 2000 through primary health care (Technical Report Series, No 717). New York: World Health Organization.

World Health Organization. (2005). Mental Health and Working Life. *WHO European Ministerial Conference on Mental Health*. Retrieved December 26, 2011, from http://apps.who.int/gb/bd/PDF/bd47/EN/constitution-en.pdf

Wright, T. A., & Bonett, D. G. (1997). The role of pleasantness and activation-based well-being in performance prediction. *Journal of Occupational Health Psychology, 2*, 212–219.

Wright, T. A., Bonett, D. G., & Sweeney, D. A. (1993). Mental health and work performance: Results of a longitudinal field study. *Journal of Occupational and Organizational Psychology, 66*, 277–284.

Wright, T. A., & Cropanzano, R. (2000). Psychological well-being and job satisfaction as predictors of job performance. *Journal of Occupational Health Psychology, 5*(1), 84–94.

Wysocki, R. K. (2009). *Effective Project Management* (5th ed.). Indianapolis, IN: Wiley.

Young, H. M., Siegel, E. O., McCormick, W. C., Fulmer, T., Harootyan, L. K., & Dorr, D. A. (2011). Interdisciplinary collaboration in geriatrics: Advancing health for older adults. *Nursing Outlook, 59*(4), 243–250.

Zika-Viktorsson, A., Sundström, P., & Engwall, M. (2006). Project overload: An exploratory study of work and management in multi-project settings. *International Journal of Project Management, 24*, 385–394.

APPENDICES

Appendix 1

Understanding Our Statistical Indices

Our objective in this appendix is to explain in brief and simple terms the statistical indices we used throughout this book.

Coefficient Alpha: Internal Consistency

Cronbach's Alpha coefficient (α) is used in the methods sections of chapters IV and V. Cronbach's Alpha is a reliability estimate that helps indicate the score derived from a group of questions targeting a single construct represents an interpretable element about how people differ from one another on that construct (Cronbach, 1951). It is said to be *internal* because all you need to calculate this coefficient is a sample of people answering a group of questions that targets a single construct such as goal clarity. The coefficient represents *consistency* if people who believe teams goals are clear answer toward the top of the answer scale (i.e., "agree" or "strongly agree") on all questions that depict goal clarity. Similarly, there is consistency if people who feel team goals are not clear answer towards the bottom of the answer scale (i.e., "disagree" or "strongly disagree") on all questions that depict goal clarity. When there is high internal consistency, questions about goal clarity can help distinguish those that are high on goal clarity from those that are not. If people who feel team goals are clear yet answer inconsistently (sometimes high, sometimes low), the group of items is likely defective. The coefficient can vary from minus infinity to 1 (although negative alphas are an oddity). To interpret the alpha coefficient, remember that the closer the number is to 1.00, the better the group of questions (Nunnally & Bernstein, 1994); there are no cutoff scores (Lance, Butts, & Michels, 2006). In the case of goal clarity at time 2, the alpha is 0.92.

Pearson's Correlation Coefficient: How Variables are Related

The correlation coefficient (r) is used in the results sections of chapters IV and V. Developed by Pearson over a century ago (Pearson, 1896), it expresses the extent to which two measures co-vary. Variance occurs when there is a variety of scores stemming from a sample of people on a measure such as goal clarity; if everybody in a sample would answer "3" (or "1" or "5," for that matter) to all items depicting goal clarity, there would be no variance. In the case of Figure 2, scores on goal clarity vary between 3 and 5; that is between neutrality and complete agreement. Variance also occurs when the same people answer

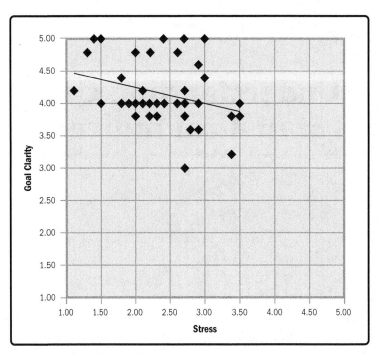

Figure 2: Graph of a co-variation

questions on another measure such as stress have scores that vary from person to person. In the case of the Figure 2, stress varies between 1.10 and 3.50. Each dot on the graph represents one person with a score on stress and a score on goal clarity. The line is drawn such that it is the closest to all dots on the graph. A line drown anywhere else on the graph would not be as close to all the dots. The line points downward indicating that as stress increases, goal clarity decreases. The line actually shows that average impact of stress on goal clarity. We can see from the graph that, on average, each increase of 1 unit of stress (say from *relatively often* to *often*) decreases goal clarity by about 0.25 units. This is apparent when looking on the downward line where stress varies between 2.00 and 3.00 and looking at how much goal clarity decreases. When stress is at 2.00, goal clarity is at 4.25. When stress is at 3.00, goal clarity is at 4.00. This line in fact is a graphical representation of a correlation coefficient. The line you see in the figure corresponds to a negative correlation of $r = -.31$, meaning increases in one measure implies a decrease in the other. Interestingly, flipping the measures on the graph (i.e., depicting goal clarity horizontally and stress vertically) would produce another downward pointing line corresponding to $r = -.31$. All it would mean is that each increase of one unit on goal clarity (say from *neutral* to *agree*) corresponds, on average, to about a 0.36 decrease on stress frequency. The correlation coefficient is a great way to summarize any co-variation between measures without having to draw a graph.

Because a correlation is a standardized index, it always and only varies between -1.00 and $+1.00$. When correlations are positive, lines in graphs point upward, meaning that increases in one measure correspond to increases in the other. A correlation of $r = .00$

means that there is no co-variation between two measures, and in that case the line would be completely horizontal. The size of the correlation increases as it departs from $r = .00$ in either direction.

Two points need to be clear when examining correlations. First, they do not convey cause-and-effect relationships. The graph you see does not mean that stress causes goals to be clearer or that clear goals causes stress to decrease. It is worth pointing out that in our study, many measures are separated in time by weeks, even months. This is why there is a slight *causal flavor* to the interpretation of a correlation coefficient when measures are separated by time, since measures taken in the past are a logical contender for predicting measures taken later, whereas the contrary is illogical.

Second, since the correlation can go right up to 1.00 (or as far down as −1.00), people tend to misinterpret correlations that are not close to these extremes. Jacob Cohen (1988) devised guidelines to help interpret correlations. He explains that a correlation of about $r = .10$ (or of about $r = −.10$) is considered small, a correlation of about $r = .30$ (or of about $r = −.30$) is of moderate size and then a correlation is about $r = .50$ (or $r = −.50$) it is considered large. To put this into context, Rosenthal and Rubin (1982) demonstrate mathematically how correlation coefficients can be understood in medical terms when comparing a treatment group who receives a medication to a control group that does not. Taking Cohen's convention of small, moderate, and large and using Rosenthal and Rubin examples, we can say that a small correlation of $r = .10$ corresponds to a situation where only 10% of the people in the treatment group feel better with the medication and only 10% of the people in the control group feel the same as before. In such a case, people in both these two groups would be pretty similar and thus the treatment would not be seen as very effective. A "moderate" correlation of $r = .30$ corresponds to a situation where 65% of the people in the treatment group feel better and 65% of the people in the control group feel the same as before; a tremendous improvement. Finally, a "large" a correlation of $r = .50$ corresponds to a situation where 75% of the people in the treatment group feel better and 75% of the people in the control group feel the same as before. Taking this to the extreme, a correlation of $r = 1.00$ would mean that 100% of the people in the treatment group would feel better and 100% of the control group would not feel any change; a very unlikely event.

For more on correlations, please consult an introductory statistics textbook.

Alpha Level: Statistical Risk Management

The alpha level (p) accompanies correlations and thus is used in the results sections of chapters 4 and 5. The *p-level* is not an index of magnitude, rather it is a number that represents the risk of making a mistake when saying that a correlation of $r = −.31$ is far enough from 0 that we can say it is not 0^2. Although it is often set at $p \leq 0.05$, choosing the *p-level* is strictly a matter of convention, not relevance (J. Cohen, 1992). For example, it is perfectly acceptable to display $p \leq 0.1$ as we did in our tables along other *p-levels*. What must be understood is that the level of risk, the size of the correlation, and the *p-level*

---

[2]This refers to Type I error. Another form of risk is Type II error. However, we will not discuss it except to say it is set at 0.80 in this example. See J. Cohen 1992 for more details.

are intimately related to the number of people in the sample (J. Cohen, 1994). Hence, a small correlation of $r = .10$ can be declared "statistically different from 0" at $p \leq 0.05$ with 783 people in the sample. Similarly, the same correlation of $r = .10$ would require a sample of 1163 to be declared "statistically different from 0" at $p \leq 0.01$. Except for the sample size, there is no difference between the two correlations. One is not less of a correlation than the other, as both result from the same calculations. In both cases, $r = .10$ is unlikely to depict a pertinent increase of one measure over another, no matter how many people in the sample. A similar reasoning is possible with larger correlations. For example, a moderate correlation of $r = .30$ with a sample of 125 would be declared "statistically different from 0" at $p \leq 0.01$, but it would take only 85 people to declare it "statistically different from 0" at $p \leq 0.05$. The main point here is that the three most important pieces of information to interpret a correlation are: (a) Does the correlation carry meaning when depicting co-variation?; (b) Is the sample representative of the population it wishes to generalize to?; and (c) What is the risk in making a mistake when declaring (or not) whether the correlation is different from 0 (or not)?

For more on *p-levels*, please consult an introductory statistics textbook. For discussions on statistical power, please read J. Cohen (1992).

Appendix 2

Training Efficacy
Component Questionnaires

This appendix is <u>not</u> the actual form presented to participants. Rather, this appendix is designed to inform researchers and practitioners of our items and methods should they want to used them or should they want to know, for example, which item belongs to which dimension. Although the English versions of our instruments and items are shown here, please note that we conducted our study in French. Psychometric properties of the French version of the instruments and items are shown in Chapter 4.

Training self-efficacy was assessed with two strategies and a pre-post design. The first strategy was to state our learning objectives in terms of actionable behaviors from which self-efficacy ratings can be generated. In doing so, we followed Bandura's (2006) recommendation for developing self-efficacy scales. Ratings of each behavior/learning objective for each workshop stem from the same instructions: *Please evaluate your confidence level as to your ability to carry out the following activities, by assigning each activity a number between 0% and 100%*. The pre-workshop form showed only the behaviors/learning objectives specific to the workshop participants were attending. Immediately after the workshop, the same behaviors/learning objectives and instructions were presented on a new form and participants had to provide new ratings. In addition to self-efficacy ratings drawn from workshop objectives, the post-workshop form also had a 15-item scale measuring training efficacy adapted by Beaulieu (in progress) from works of Rivard (2006) and Saks and Haccoun (2010).

Self-Efficacy
Pre-post Self-Efficacy Behaviors (by the authors of this book)

Learning objectives for Workshop 1

1. Identify the main element that distinguishes project work from other forms of work.
2. Identify each element of the triple constraint.
3. Identify the types of decisions that occur at the beginning of a project and those that occur at the end.
4. Understand the difference between a formal role and an informal role.
5. Become aware of roles you can play on your team.
6. Start putting together your project charter.

Items under "Human factors": 4,5.
Items under "Project management factors : 1–3, 6.

Learning objectives for Workshop 2

1. Invest yourself in the project, despite the constraints.
2. Negotiate your expectations with other teammates.
3. Interact with your teammates to maximize the contribution of each.
4. Understanding your involvement and that of others in each of the tasks of the project.
5. Identify tasks that are critical to the project.
6. Estimate the duration of a group of dependent tasks.
7. Begin the detailed plan of your project.

Items under "Human factors": 1–4.
Items under "Project management factors": 5–7.

Learning objectives for Workshop 3

1. Identify risks to the project.
2. Propose solutions to manage risks.
3. Analyze the relevance of changes to the project.
4. Establish individual goals that aim to improve the efficiency of the team.
5. Take measures to improve the efficiency of the team.

Items under "Human factors": 4,5.
Items under "Project management factors": 1–3.

Satisfaction and Transferability

Post-Workshop Satisfaction and Transferability Questionnaire (Beaulieu, in progress)

Please rate the extent to which you agree with each of statements using the following scale

1 = Strongly disagree
2 = Disagree
3 = Neither disagree nor agree
4 = Agree
5 = Strongly agree

1. The content of the workshop corresponded to my needs and concerns.
2. The objectives of the workshop were, in my opinion, met.
3. The training techniques employed facilitated learning.
4. There was a good balance between theory and practical content.
5. The documentation was well written and will be otherwise useful to me.
6. The exercises and activities suggested were relevant to the workshop.
7. The trainers were well prepared and organized.
8. The trainers knew their subject well.
9. The trainers communicated clearly and were dynamic.
10. The trainers facilitated discussions and participation from the group.

11. The trainers clearly answered all my questions.
12. The examples given by the trainers were relevant and sufficient in number.
13. The discussions between participants were rich in information and contributed to my learning.
14. The length of the workshop was neither too long, nor too short.
15. This workshop allowed me to increase my knowledge and learn new things.
16. The knowledge acquired during the workshop can be directly applied to my job.
17. I plan on utilizing this new knowledge in my work.
18. The content and examples given during the workshop were representative of my work context.
19. On the whole, the knowledge acquired in this workshop will be useful to me.
20. I would recommend this workshop to my work colleagues.

Items under "Satisfaction with training": 1–14, 20.
Items under "Transferability of knowledge acquired": 15–19.

Appendix 3

Workload, Demands, Control and Stress Component Questionnaires

This appendix is <u>not</u> the actual form presented to participants. Rather, it is designed to inform researchers and practitioners of our items and methods should they want to used them or should they want to know, for example, which item belongs to which dimension. All instruments are referenced and, except where mentioned otherwise, they are in the public domain. Most instruments and/or answer scales were adapted somewhat to our context. For copyrighted instruments, we obtained permission to use and only excerpts are shown here. Although the English versions of our instruments and items are shown here, please note that we conducted our study in French. Psychometric properties of the French version of the instruments and items are shown in Chapter 5.

For questionnaire A, participants were instructed to answer questions while *referring to their present work environment*[3]. For questionnaire B, participants were instructed to answer in terms of *in the last month*. For questionnaires A and B, participants had to answer using one of three response formats[4].

- Agreement response format asked to choose one number according to the following scale: 1 = Strongly disagree; 2 = Disagree; 3 = Neither disagree nor agree; 4 = Agree; 5 = Strongly agree.
- Frequency response format suggested the following choices: 1 = Never or almost never; 2 = Occasionally; 3 = Relatively often; 4 = Often; 5 = Very often.
- Self-efficacy response format provided the following instructions: Rate your confidence level as to your ability to perform the following activities by assigning each activity any number between 0% and 100%.

In the following pages, each instrument will be presented, including original authors, which of the three response formats applies, and for multiple dimension instruments, which item belongs to which dimension. Please note items identified with "r" require reversing participants' responses before calculating the score.

---

[3]Except for social support, where instructions were *when you have conflicts at work*.
[4]Except for the Project Involvement Index, which simply requires a number entered for each question.

Questionnaire A (Time 0)

Preference for Group Work (Campion et al., 1993) (Agreement Response Format)

1. If given the choice, I would prefer to work as part of a team rather than work alone.
2. I find that working as a member of a team increases my ability to perform effectively.
3. I generally prefer to work as part of a team.

Supporting Infrastructure (Spreitzer, 1996) (Agreement Response Format)

1. When I need additional resources to do my job, I can usually get them.
2. I have access to the resources I need to do my job well.
3. I can obtain the resources necessary to support new ideas.

Project Management Maturity (Kerzner, 1998) (Agreement Response Format)

1. My organization recognizes the need for project management. This need is recognized at all levels of management, including senior management.
2. My organization has a system in place to manage both cost and schedule. The system requires charge numbers and cost account codes. The systems reports variances from planned targets.
3. My organization has recognized the benefits that are possible from implementing project management. These benefits have been recognized at all levels of management, including senior management.
4. My organization has a well-defined project management methodology using life-cycle phases.
5. Our executives visibly support project management through executive presentations, correspondence, and by occasionally attending project teams meetings or briefings.
6. My organization is committed to quality up-front planning. We try to do the best we can at planning.
7. Our lower- and middle-level line managers totally and visibly support the project management process.
8. My organization is doing everything possible to minimize "creeping" scope (i.e., scope changes) on our products.
9. The executives in my organization have a good understanding of the principles of project management.
10. Our lower- and middle-level line managers have been trained and educated in project management.
11. Our executives have recognized or identified the applications of project management of various parts of our business.
12. My organization has successfully integrated cost and schedule control together for both managing projects and reporting status.
13. My organization has developed a project management curriculum (i.e., more than one or two courses) to enhance the project the project management skills of our employees.

14. Our lower- and middle-level line managers are willing to release their employees for project management training.
15. Our executives have demonstrated a willingness to change our way of doing business in order to mature in project management.

Items under "Embryonic maturity": items 1, 3, 11.
Items under "Executive maturity": 5, 9.
Items under "Line management maturity": 7, 14.
Items under "Growth maturity": 4, 6, 8.
Items under "Maturity": 2, 12, 13.

Conflict Handling (De Dreu et al., 2001) (Frequency Response Format)

1. I give in to the wishes of the other party.
2. I concur with the other party.
3. I try to accommodate the other party.
4. I adapt to the other parties' goals and interests.
5. I try to realize a middle-of-the-road solution.
6. I emphasize that we have to find a compromise solution.
7. I insist we both give in a little.
8. I strive whenever possible towards a 50–50 compromise.
9. I push my own point of view.
10. I search for gains.
11. I fight for a good outcome for myself.
12. I do everything to win.
13. I examine issues until I find a solution that really satisfies me and the other party.
14. I stand for my own and other's goals and interests.
15. I examine ideas from both sides to find a mutually optimal solution.
16. I work out a solution that serves my own as well as other's interests as good as possible.
17. I avoid a confrontation about our differences.
18. I avoid differences of opinion as much as possible.
19. I try to make differences loom less severe.
20. I try to avoid a confrontation with the other.

Items under "Yielding": 1–4.
Items under "Compromising": 5–8.
Items under "Forcing: items": 9–12.
Items under "Problem solving": 13–16.
Items under "Avoiding": 17–20.

Informational Role Self-Efficacy (Chiocchio, Dubé, et al., 2012) (Self-efficacy Response Format)

1. Build on my area of expertise to enrich team discussions
2. Improve teamwork by interventions that showcase my professional expertise
3. Clarify the nature of my professional expertise with team members

4. Advise team members by integrating the specifics of my area of expertise
5. Show the contribution of my area of expertise when the team needs to solve a problem

Questionnaire B (Times 1 and 2)

Project Involvement Index (Chiocchio et al., 2010)

1. Thinking of your work in the last month, indicate the number of projects on which you have worked: _____.
2. Thinking of your work in the last month, indicate the percentage of your time you have spent on one or more projects: _____.

Job Demands (Bosma et al., 1997) (Frequency Response Format)

1. I must work very fast.
2. I must work very intensely.
3. I have enough time to do everything. (r)
4. Different groups at work demand things from me that I think are hard to combine.

Job Control (Bosma et al., 1997) (Frequency Response Format)

1. I have a choice in deciding how to do my job.
2. I have a choice in deciding what I do at work.
3. Others make decisions concerning my work.
4. I have a good deal of say in decisions about my work.
5. I have a say in my own work speed.
6. My working time can be flexible.
7. I can decide when to take a break.
8. I have a say in choosing with whom I work.
9. I have a great deal of say in planning my work.
10. I have to do the same thing over and over again (r)
11. My job provides me with a variety of interesting things to do.
12. My job is boring (r).
13. I have the possibility of learning new things through my work.
14. My work demands a high level of skill or expertise.
15. My job requires me to take the initiative.

Items under "Decision Authority": 1–9.
Items under "Skill Discretion": 10–15.

Perceived Stress (S. Cohen et al., 1983) (Frequency Response Format)

1. In the last month, how often have you been upset because of something that happened unexpectedly?
2. In the last month, how often have you felt that you were unable to control the important things in your life?
3. In the last month, how often have you felt nervous and "stressed"?
4. In the last month, how often have you felt confident about your ability to handle your personal problems? (r)

5. In the last month, how often have you felt that things were not going your way?[5]
6. In the last month, how often have you found that you could not cope with all the things that you had to do?
7. In the last month, how often have you been able to control irritations in your life? (r)
8. In the last month, how often have you felt that you were on top of things? (r)
9. In the last month, how often have you been angered because of things that were outside of your control?
10. In the last month, how often have you felt difficulties were piling up so high that you could not overcome them?

Anxiety (Stride, Wall, & Catley, 2007; Warr, 2005) (Frequency Response Format)

1. How many times your job made you feel tense.
2. How many times your job made you feel calm (r)
3. How many times your job made you feel relaxed (r)
4. How many times your job made you feel worried
5. How many times your job made you feel anxious

Depression (Stride et al., 2007; Warr, 2005) (Frequency Response Format)

1. How many times your job made you feel miserable.
2. How many times your job made you feel depressed.
3. How many times your job made you feel optimistic. (r)
4. How many times your job made you feel enthusiastic. (r)
5. How many times your job made you feel gloomy.
6. How many times your job made you feel motivated. (r)

Goal Similarity (Jehn, 1995) (Agreement Response Format)

1. In my project team, we have similar goals.
2. The main goals of my project team are the same for all members.
3. We (my project team) all agree upon what is important for our group.

Task Interdependency (Campion et al., 1993) (Agreement Response Format)

1. I cannot accomplish my tasks without information or materials from other members of my team.
2. Other members of my team depend on me for information or materials needed to perform their tasks.
3. Within my team, jobs performed by team members are related to one another.

Goal Clarity (Sawyer, 1992) (Agreement Response Format)

1. My duties and responsibilities are clear to me.
2. The goals and objectives for my job are clear.

---

[5]A problem during translation occurred so that this question should have been worded as "In the last month, how often have you felt that things were going your way?" and then reversed-scored. The way we used it, however, did not modify the integrity of the construct.

3. It is clear how my work relates to the overall objectives of my project team.
4. The expected results of my work are clear.
5. It is clear what aspects of my work will lead to positive evaluations.

Intra-Team Trust (Simons & Peterson, 2000) (Agreement Response Format)

1. We absolutely respect each other's competence.
2. Every team member shows absolute integrity.
3. We expect the complete truth from each other.
4. We are all certain that we can fully trust each other.
5. We count on each other to fully live up to our word.

Project Commitment (Hoegl et al., 2004) (Agreement Response Format)

1. Our project team feels fully responsible for achieving the common project goals.
2. This project has the strong commitment of our team members.
3. The team members are proud to be part of the project.
4. The team members are committed not only to their teams, but to the overall project.
5. Our team values to be part of this project.

Social Provision Scale (Cutrona & Russell, 1987) (Agreement Response Format)

This instrument is protected by copyright, so only a sample of the 24 items are shown. Written permission was obtained for use in the study.

- There is someone I could talk to about important decisions in my life.
- There are people I can depend on to help me if I really need it.
- I have relationships where my competence and skill are recognized.
- I feel personally responsible for the well-being of another person.
- I feel a strong emotional bond with at least one other person.
- There are people who enjoy the same social activities I do.

Collaboration (Chiocchio, Grenier, et al., 2012) (Frequency Response Format)

My teammates and I. . .

1. ... provide each other with useful information that makes work progress.
2. ... share knowledge that promotes work progress.
3. ... understand each other when we talk about the work to be done.
4. ... share resources that help perform tasks.
5. ... communicate our ideas to each other about the work to be done.
6. ... carry out our tasks at the appropriate moment.
7. ... make sure our tasks are completed on time.
8. ... make adjustments in order to meet deadlines.
9. ... make progress reports.
10. ... exchange information on "who does what."
11. ... discuss work deadlines with each other.
12. ... can foresee each other's needs without having to express them.

13. ... instinctively reorganize our tasks when changes are required.
14. ... have an implicit understanding of the assigned tasks.

Items under "Teamwork communication": 1–5.
Items under "Synchronicity": 6–8.
Items under "Explicit Coordination": 9–11.
Items under "Implicit Coordination": 12–14.

Interdisciplinary Collaboration (Vinokur-Kaplan, 1995) (Agreement Response Format)

1. Suggestions from other team members have improved my effectiveness in working in this setting.
2. After an issue is raised, we quickly reach a decision as to what to do about it.
3. Team decisions are controlled by one or two individuals. (r)
4. Exposure to the role of other disciplines has increased my awareness of their contribution the treatment process.
5. Before undertaking a course of action, team members rarely ask for help and suggestions from others.
6. Working closely with other team members has helped in developing skills I might not have learned working with people in my own professional discipline.
7. My team meetings focus on clearly defined issues.
8. There is a low degree of participation on the part of some members of the team. (r)
9. Members of the team work together as a team.
10. Members do not discuss some the important problems they are confronted with because the other professional discipline would not fully understand the problems. (r)

Conflits (De Dreu & Van Vianen, 2001; Jehn & Mannix, 2001) (Frequency Response Format)

How frequently. . .

1. ... does your team experience interpersonal relationship tensions?
2. ... does your team experience manifestations of anger?
3. ... does your team experience emotional conflict?
4. ... does your team experience conflict regarding ideas?
5. ... does your team experience disagreements about the task to accomplish?
6. ... does your team experience conflicting opinions about the project?
7. ... does your team experience disagreements about "who" does "what"?
8. ... does your team experience conflict regarding task responsibilities?
9. ... does your team experience disagreements about resource allocation?

Items under "Relationship conflict": 1–3.
Items under "Task conflict": 4–6.
Items under "Process conflict": 7–9.

Behavioral Performance (Griffin et al., 2007) (Frequency Response Format)

1. I carry out the core parts of my job well.
2. I complete my core tasks well using the standard procedures.
3. I ensure my tasks are completed properly.

4. I adapt well to changes in core tasks.
5. I cope with changes to the way I have to do my core tasks.
6. I learn new skills to help me adapt to changes in my tasks.
7. I initiate better ways of doing my core tasks.
8. I come up with ideas to improve the way in which my core tasks are done.
9. I make changes to the way my core tasks are done.
10. I coordinate my work with coworkers.
11. I communicate effectively with my coworkers.
12. I provide help to coworkers when asked, or needed.
13. I deal effectively with changes affecting my team (e.g., new members).
14. I learn new skills or take on new roles to cope with changes in the way my team works.
15. I respond constructively to changes in the way my team works.
16. I suggest ways to make my team more effective.
17. I develop new and improved methods to help my team perform better.
18. I improve the way my team does things.

Items under "Individual taskwork": 1–3.
Items under "Individual adaptability": 4–6.
Items under "Individual proactivity": 7–9.
Items under "Team taskwork": 10–12.
Items under "Team adaptability": 13–15.
Items under "Team proactivity": 16–18.

Regular Assessment of Project (Stratman & Roth, 2002) (Agreement Response Format)

1. We constantly review our project capabilities against strategic goals.
2. The project plans are redesigned as required to meet evolving conditions.
3. Strategic project planning is a continuous process.
4. The project tasks are reviewed on a periodic basis.

Project Performance (Gelbard & Carmeli, 2009) (Agreement Response Format)

So far. . .

1. ... this project met the planned schedule.
2. ... this project was conducted within the allocated working hours.
3. ... this project met the planned budget framework.
4. ... this project completely met all customer specifications.
5. ... it appears that this project will produce a high quality service/product.
6. ... what needed to be delivered was delivered on time.
7. ... this project didn't have time (working hours) overrun.
8. ... this project didn't have budget overrun.
9. ... all specified functional requirements were completely met.
10. ... all project specifications were attained.

Items under "Budget and Time": 1–3, 6–8.
Items under "Functional": 4, 5, 9, 10.

Appendix 4

Demands, Control and Stress Component Interview

The following questions present an outline of the semi-structured interview. Original questions were asked in French. More information on the interview process is presented in Chapter 6.

1. Introduction to the interview
   a. Greetings; Express gratitude for participation
   b. Explain interview:
      i. Objective (Evolution of human relations exploration in work team situation regarding recognition, autonomy and power dynamics)
      ii. Purpose within the research project
      iii. Duration: 45–60 minutes
      iv. 4 parts (review of the project, of the project team, of the participant's role within the team and comments).
   c. Obtain participant's consent regarding the audio recording (anonymity and confidentiality issues, recording procedures, and note-taking during the interview)
2. Content of interview
   a. Part 1 – Review of the project
      i. Could you tell us about your project in general?
      ii. What did you think of the project?
      iii. How did you get involved in the project?
      iv. Could you tell us about your level of satisfaction with the outcome of your project?
      v. In your opinion, in what ways did the workshops influence or not the completion of your project?
      vi. To what extent did leadership style influence the outcome of your project?
      vii. In instances when the project created a source of joy or suffering, how did this translate?
      viii. Which strategies were used to reduce, avoid, or eliminate sources of suffering during the project? In what ways were these strategies effective in reducing suffering?
   b. Part 2 – Review of the project team
      i. Could you tell us about your project team and how it works?
      ii. Concretely, how was the work carried out?

iii. How did you get involved in the team?

iv. How did relationships develop during the project?

v. Were you able to meet your teammates demands?

vi. In your opinion, how can the outcome of your work be explained? The performance of your team?

vii. What sort of tensions or conflicts influenced team functioning? How?

viii. To what extent did the leadership style of the person in charge influence the team's operation?

ix. What were sources of joy (for example, opportunities for growth, recognition, visibility,..) and sources of suffering (for example, excessive stress, conditions hindering personal growth or development of competencies, lack of recognition or autonomy, alienation, etc.)?

x. What strategies were used to reduce, avoid, or eliminate sources of suffering throughout the project? How effective were these strategies?

c. Part 3 – Review of your role within the team

i. Could you tell us about the role(s) you played within this team?

ii. What influence do you believe to have had on the outcome of your project? (Address the positive and negative effects)

iii. What influence do you believe to have had on the operation of your team? (Address the positive and negative effects)

iv. What influence do you believe to have had on the relationship among team members during the project? (Address the positive and negative effects)

v. What are the main emotions you experienced during the project?

vi. In what ways did the way of working in a team offer (or not) possibilities for self-actualization and the development of skills?

d. Part 4 – Comments

i. Do you have any other comments to make regarding your project, its outcome, and team functioning?

ii. What do you believe to have learned about yourself after the completion of this team project?

iii. In your opinion, would you do this experience over? Why?

iv. If possible, what would you do differently when working on future projects?

3. End of the interview

a. Express thanks. Re-state anonymity and confidentiality of interview materials.

b. Answer interviewee questions, if any.

Appendix 5

Project Charter Template

SCOPE STATEMENT COMPONENTS (Use this structure to create your scope statement)	
Structural Elements	**Detail**
The problem is that	• Describe the problems the outcome of the project should help address
Project name	• Give a name to your project
Aims at	• Choose an action verb : (e.g., create, design, develop, improve, deliver, evaluate, establish, etc.) and • Describe the service / product that will be the result of the project
In order to	• Describe anticipated benefits of the service / product
Before	• Determine a final date for project completion

SCOPE STATEMENT
Given **the problem is that** (...), the (**project name**) project **aims at** (...) **in order to** (...) **before** (...).

TEAM MEMBERS		
Name	**Expertise**	**Coordinates***
Name 1	• [describe expertise here]	• Phone: • Fax: • Cellular: • Pager: • Email:
Name 2	• [describe expertise here]	• Phone: • Fax: • Cellular: • Pager: • Email:
Etc.		

Note: *Indicates preferred means of communication.

ROLES AND RESPONSIBILITIES			
Name	**Project Responsibilities**	**Formal Role**	**Informal Role**
Name 1	• [describe responsibilities here]	• [describe formal role here]	• [describe informal role here]
Name 2	• [describe responsibilities here]	• [describe formal role here]	• [describe informal role here]
Etc.			

STAKEHOLDERS AND REQUIREMENTS		
People, groups, entities, organizations, etc., affected by the process and/or the outcome of the project	**Stakeholders' requirements regarding the project's process**	**Stakeholders' requirements regarding the project's outcome**
Stakeholder 1	[insert requirement(s) here] ▶ [describe measure(s) that will demonstrate if/how requirement(s) will be met]	[insert requirement(s) here] ▶ [describe measure(s) that will demonstrate if/how requirement(s) will be met]
Stakeholder 2	[insert requirement(s) here] ▶ [describe measure(s) that will demonstrate if/how requirement(s) will be met]	[insert requirement(s) here] ▶ [describe measure(s) that will demonstrate if/how requirement(s) will be met]
Etc.		

PHASES AND MILESTONES	
Phase Name	**Milestone**
Phase 1	• [describe state that must be reached]
Phase 2	• [describe state that must be reached]
Etc.	

Appendix 6

Activity Planning Template

Task Number:	Start Date: / /	**Estimated Duration in Days**

Estimated Duration in Days
Optimistic: _____
Realistic: _____
Pessimistic: _____

End Date: /   /

Task Description: _____
_____
_____
_____

Task:
☐ Important but not critical
☐ Critical to the process (deadline/cost)
☐ Critical to the result (quality)

In Charge of this Task (Implication) *
_____ (___)
_____ (___)
_____ (___)
_____ (___)

Concerned Parties (How) *
_____ (___)
_____ (___)
_____ (___)
_____ (___)

Dependence:
☐ None
☐ To begin, task _____ must be complete
☐ To begin, task _____ must be underway

Who will determine the success of this task, and how?
_____
_____
_____

*Legend
Implication: The people in charge must do, help, advise, verify quality, control progression, etc.
How: The concerned parties will need to be consulted, present, informed of the progression, etc.

Appendix 7

Risk Analysis Template

Step 1– Individually

Take time individually to list all the events and situations you can think could negatively affect your project. Think of what could diminish the quality of the outcome, cause a setback/delay, or cause you to invest more time than necessary. Work individually and do not consult with others; simply express in your own words risks you are worried about.

STEP 1
Individual List of Risks

Step 2– As a Team

Discuss as a team the risks you have thought of in step 1. Clean the list to ensure there are no duplicates. It is important that everybody's risks are listed, so be careful not to eliminate any risks at this stage. Discuss in sufficient detail so that all team members understand all risks listed.

Step 3– Individually

Once the team has an official list of risks, take time individually to indicate if the probability of each risk occurring is low, moderate or high, and indicate if, in your opinion, the impact of this risk would be small, moderate, or large should it occur. Work individually and do not consult with others; simply mark all risks to the best of your ability.

Step 4– As a Team

As a team, discuss each element from step 3 (probability and impact) in order to reach a consensus. The objective of this last step is to agree on the "official" probability and impact scores that your team will attribute to each of the risks. Try to avoid simply averaging the scores across team members. Rather, make sure everybody has an opportunity to discuss the reasons behind their scores. Listen carefully and respectfully to the points of view of others and adjust your views if needed. When you have reached a team consensus on the scores for a risk, mark it down in the table below, multiply the probability score with the

STEP 2	STEP 3						STEP 4
"Clean" List of Risks	Probability of the Risk Occurring			Impact on the Project if Risk Occurs			Risk Index (multiply Probability score with Impact score)
	1 = Low	2 = Moderate	3 = High	1 = Small	2 = Moderate	3 = Large	

impact score for each risk, and write the result in the risk index column for the risk. Repeat for all risks. Then, rank the order of risks using the risk index column.

Step 5– As a Team

Starting from the risk with the highest risk index, work your way down and keep all the risks the team feels necessary to develop a plan for. As a rule of thumb, the number of risks should not be less that the top 20%, and usually does not exceed the top 50%. For each risk selected, determine if this risk must be prevented, controlled, or accepted by referring to the following definitions:

- Prevent a risk. Preventing a risk means that the team operates at the source of risk to reduce its probability. How to control this risk therefore lies in actions undertaken to reduce the likelihood of the risk occurring.
- Control a risk. Controlling a risk means that the team is taking steps to reduce the negative consequences of the risk to a level that is acceptable. How to control this risk therefore lies in actions undertaken to reduce the potential impact of risk.
- Accept a risk. Accepting a risk means that the team is aware of the existence of the risk, but chooses not to take any special measures to prevent it or control it. This option recognizes that some risks are not worth planning for it at this time. If they occur, the team will need to allocate more time and more resources; these should be set aside.

STEP 5 – RISK PLAN			
Risk	Should this risk be prevented? If yes, say how.	Should this risk be controlled? If yes, say how.	Should this risk be accepted? If yes, say how.
Risk 1			
Risk 2			
Etc.			

Appendix 8

Multi-Sources Feedback Report

Feedback report
ID number
99999

(this report is basd on fictitious data and is for illustration purposes only)

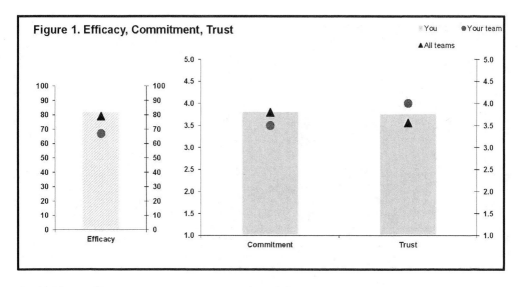

Figure 1. Efficacy, Commitment, Trust

Informational role self-efficacy

Informational role self-efficacy is an individual's capability beliefs in exteriorizing his/her informational characteristics pertinent to other's task performance. You've rated highly on this dimension. You attach importance to build on you area of expertise to enrich team discussions. You are confident in your capability to enrich team discussions. When the team needs to solve a problem, you clearly show the contribution of your expertise and experience.

Commitment to the project

The commitment to the project is the degree of commitment and identification of each team member to the objectives and outcomes. A successful team is a team that is strongly committed to its purpose, objectives, methods and towards his teammates. You have rated your team listed favorably in terms of commitment to the project. Depending on your perspective, your team members have taken on the project, appreciate it and are proud to work on it. Keep an eye on this. Act quickly if you see a member of the team losing commitment - discuss the events and situations that caused it so that others may not be affected. Acknowledge, encourage and celebrate the "small victories" as they arise.

Intra-team trust

Intra-team trust is the impression that the team is able to complete the project, to do what is best for the team and their teammates. Trust is built from the experiences of the team. When a team overcomes obstacles and challenges successfully, the members are more confident and believe more in their abilities to each other. They give themselves encouragement to act toward the achievement of team objectives before individual goals. You listed your team favorably on intra-team trust. Still, stay on the lookout for potential fluctuations on the subject. Ensure that the individual commitments that contributed to progress on the project are highlighted.

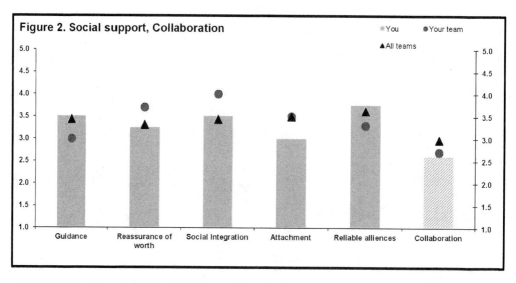

Figure 2. Social support, Collaboration

Social support is a set of resources that we enjoy through our relationships with others. Social support allows us to feel adequate and to avoid loneliness when we are faced with a difficult situation.

Guidance

Ability of others to provide us with advice or relevant information when we are in "problem solving" mode. You have rated your team low on this dimension. Let it be known should you need advice or information when you are in "problem solving" mode.

Reassurance of worth

Feeling that others recognize your value, our skills and abilities. You feel that your team members do not recognize your skills and abilities. They may not perceive it. Make sure your behavior (actions or words) actually reflect the contributions you capable of. Redefine as necessary the division of roles (formal and informal) and responsibilities in relation to the mandate.

Social Integration

Feeling that we belong to a team whose members share similar interests, common concerns and similar recreational activities. You feel that the team members are disparate in terms of their interests, concerns and activities. Discuss this topic during a team meeting. Revisit the mandate and make sure everybody understands it the same way. If the project mandate does not need to be changed, check to what extent the behavior of each member was used to reach the goal. If the mandate should be changed, please clarify this with all team members and the other parties involved.

Attachment

Impression of emotional closeness from which one draws a sense of security. You do not really feel attached to your team. It may be that you do not see the climate as "safe" to openly discuss issues. Make sure that this impression is not hiding too much timidity on your part. Also make sure that this impression does not interfere with the progress of the project or goals.

Reliable alliances

Feeling that you can rely on others, that they can help you solve a concrete problem. You rated this dimension positively. This means that you feel that you are helping others at the right time, when needed. Be sure to do the same for others by asking questions and offering your help.

Collaborative practice is an interprofessional process of communication and decision making that creates a synergy of knowledge and skills specific to each person in order to advance the project.

Interprofessional collaboration

Collaboration is important in your team because it is an indicator of efficiency. You rated this dimension as low. You feel that the knowledge and skills of team members are not properly used, that decisions are not always made collectively. You feel that the participation and exchanges do not always allow to clearly identify a problem or to distribute the responsibilities of each member. You can help improve the situation by communicating and interacting more regularly with colleagues. Tell them your specific discipline and area of practice. Ask them about their own and discuss the interdependencies between disciplines that can advance the project. Ask those who rarely speak up.

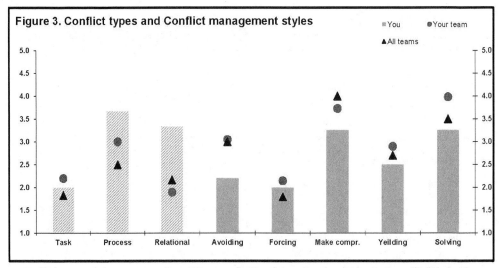

Figure 3. Conflict types and Conflict management styles

Conflicts emanate from a perception of incompatibility of views and involve behaviours that disrupt team functioning. They vary in intensity from simple disagreements to paralyzing clashes and disputes.

Task conflict

Task conflict involves different views about the necessary tasks required to move the project forward. You rated your team favorably on this. You seem to share similar views in terms of tasks. This is good news if the project is progressing well, since it means that the discussions you have appeared to lead to doing the right things the right way. However, if the project is not progressing well, you should spend more time discussing tasks and express your views more often, even provoke debate. These debates - if they avoid negative affect – contribute to better group decisions.

Process conflict

Process conflict involves different views regarding the steps needed to advance the project. You think your team is having difficulties in this regard. The team members often disagree on the distribution of resources among team members and responsibilities. Try to improve communication between members and take the time to (re)define roles and expectations. Clearly define the issues regarding the responsibilities and allocation of resources and try to find, with input from others, an effective and clear way to distribute them. Do not explain the causes of disagreements with personality traits. Stay "cool" and focus on decisions about the processes that will advance the project. Make sure to leave room for other team members to express themselves on their vision. Remember that even if your views are not all adopted, the decisions taken in the end are in the best interests of the group.

Relational conflict

Relational conflicts are what people call "personality conflicts" and are not related to disagreements regarding tasks or processes. Relational conflicts involve negative affect that threatens our self-identity and our self-efficacy. You think your team is having difficulties in this regard. The team members often disagree on the distribution of resources among team members and responsibilities. Try to improve communication between members and take the time to (re) define roles and expectations. Clearly define the issues regarding the responsibilities and allocation of resources and try to find, with input from others, an effective and clear way to distribute them. Do not explain the causes of disagreements with personality traits. Stay "cool" and focus on decisions about the processes that will advance the project. Make sure to leave room for other team members to express themselves on their vision.

Your style of conflict management is the approach you prefer when you are faced with a problem. This style depends on the intensity with which you are concerned about yourself and the intensity with which you are concerned about others.

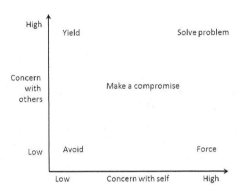

Adapted from De Dreu, et al. (2001)

Avoiding

Avoiding is an orientation where one attempts to minimize the importance of issues causing conflict and to stop thinking about these issues. This style does not seem to be your preference. Continue to avoid ... avoid it!

Forcing

Forcing is the orientation where one imposes one's will on others. This style does not seem to be your preference. This is a good thing since such an orientation would promote relationship conflict.

Make a compromise

Compromise is an orientation in which the person seeks to satisfy some of the needs of others and some of his or her own needs. This style does not seem to be your preference. On occasion, this strategy could be useful; stay attentive to compromise opportunities.

Yielding

Making concessions is a direction that will allow you to, more often than not, accept and integrate the will of others. This style does not seem to be your preference. Perfect!

Problem solving

Problem solving is an orientation where a person tries to satisfy his own aspirations as much as those of others, and involves an exchange of information on the preferences and priorities of each member, as well as negotiation. This style does not seem to be your preference. As this is the best strategy for conflict management, you should try to adopt this style. In discussions, work sessions or when a dispute arises, ask the other to express their interests, desires and feelings, while communicating your own. Learn about their perspective and give your views.

Results in table form

Figure 1.

	Effeciency	Commitment	Trust
All	67.0	3.5	4.0
Team	79.2	3.8	3.6
You	81.8	3.8	3.8

Figure 2.

	Guidance	Recog.	Social integr	Attachement	Alliances	Interprof. Collab
All	3.0	3.7	4.0	3.5	3.3	2.7
Team	3.4	3.3	3.4	3.5	3.6	3.0
You	3.5	3.3	3.5	3.0	3.8	2.6

Figure 3.

	Task	Process	Relational	Avoding	Forcing	Compromizing	Yielding	Probl. Solving
All	2.2	3.0	1.9	3.1	2.1	3.7	2.9	4.0
Team	1.8	2.5	2.2	3.0	1.8	4.0	2.7	3.5
You	2.0	3.7	3.3	2.2	2.0	3.3	2.5	3.3

References

Informational role self-efficacy: Chiocchio, F., Dubé, J-N., Lebel, P. (2012). Initial validation evidence for a short self-reported scale measuring informational role self-efficacy. Paper presented at the 73rd Annual Canadian Psychological Association convention, Halifax (NS) Canada.

Project commitment : Hoegl, M., Weinkauf, K., & Gemuenden, H. G. (2004). Interteam coordination, project commitment, and teamwork in multiteam R&D projects: A longitudinal study. Organization Science, 15(1), 38-55.

Intra-team trust : Simons, T. L., & Peterson, R. S. (2000). Task conflict and relationship conflict in top management teams: The pivotal role of intragroup trust. Journal of Applied Psychology, 85(1), 102-111.

Social support : Cutrona, C. E., & Russell, D. W. (1987). The provisions of social relationships and adaptation to stress. Advances in Personal Relationships, 1, 37-67.

Interprofessional collaboration : Vinokur-Kaplan, D. (1995). Treatment teams that work (and those that don't): An application of Hackman's Group Effectivness Model to interdisciplinary teams in psychiatric hospitals. Journal of Applied Behavioral Science, 31(3), 303-327.

Conflict : Jehn, K. A., & Mannix, E. (2001). The dynamic nature of conflict: A longitudinal study of intragroup conflict and group performance. Academy of Management Journal, 42(2), 238-251.

Conflict management style : De Dreu, C., K,W, Evers, A., Beersma, B., Kluwer, E. S., & Nauta, A. (2001). A theory-based measure of conflict management strategies in the workplace. Journal of Organizational Behavior, 22, 645-668.

Appendix 9

Study Limitations

Sample Size

As with many field studies, sample size is limited. Our study was limited to 11 teams and 76 team members. More would have been better. Small sample size causes two problems:

Varying Membership

Whether it is because the teams' membership changed along the way or whether people on these teams were too busy to attend all workshops or to respond to all three questionnaires, the sample size we had on hand to make our calculations varied. Although the *p-level* for each correlation was always commensurate with the number of people behind each correlation (see Appendix 1), the number of people varied from one correlation to another, as shown at the bottom of each table (i.e., *N*). Although it is a normal problem of project teams in the real world, in the artificial world of statistics and research, this means that there is a chance the changes in team membership is a phenomenon that affected our results, as opposed to the actual things we wanted to study, such as project workload, job control, job control, stress, collaboration, conflict, etc.

Individual versus Team Level of Analysis

Because people were embedded in teams, they shared experiences that might distinguish them from other people on other teams. Capturing team phenomena to explain why, for example, correlations between people's stress and behavioral performance differ (or not) depending on if a person is in a successful or a less successful project team, requires special statistical techniques called random coefficient modeling or hierarchical linear analysis (Raudenbush & Bryk, 2002). As for other complex techniques, these are multivariate and require a large sample size and an especially large number of teams. Interprofessional health care project teams willing to participate in a study on stress are sufficiently rare to prevent us from using this technique for the time being.

So, while we have team-level phenomena affecting our data in ways we cannot detect, we can nevertheless press on as long as we are careful when we interpret our results. For example, correlations derived from constructs that refer to individuals (e.g., see supporting infrastructure in Appendix 2 and stress in Appendix 3: all items refer to the person answering the questions) are measures easily interpreted as an individual-level phenomenon. It gets a little trickier when some measures refer to teal-level phenomena. For example, the correlation between stress (an individual-level construct) and conflict (a team-level construct; see Appendix 3) cannot be interpreted as "the correlation between stress and conflict"; this would require random coefficient modeling. Rather, it has to be interpreted as "the correlation between stress and *the perception* of conflict." There is nothing wrong with working with perceptions of team-level constructs. First, some constructs (e.g., see collaboration in Chiocchio, Grenier, et al., 2012) have validation data demonstrating that individual-level perceptions of team-level constructs behave similarly than when the construct is brought to the team-level. Second, as humans, we behave based on how we perceive our environment, so learning about perceptions carries much weight. Nevertheless, we were careful to discuss our data without making cross-level misinterpretations.

Reliability

Inter-Rater Reliability

We did not calculate indices of inter-rater reliability when examining our qualitative data. In such analyses, the researcher is not independent from data gathering and data construction.

Internal Consistency

The vast majority of internal consistency estimates for our questionnaires were adequate. Specifically, 42% of Cronbach's alphas were above .85, and 43% were between .70 and .84[6]. However, some questionnaires or dimensions of questionnaires showed questionable internal consistency, so caution must be exercised when interpreting results. Task conflict at time 1 and task and process conflict at time 2 were $\alpha = .69$, .69, and .66 respectively. Time and budget project performance at time 1 was $\alpha = .66$. Growth maturity was $\alpha = .60$ at time 0. Task interdependency at both times was $\alpha = .68$. Social support was, overall, the least internally consistent instrument. Of the 12 indices (i.e., six dimensions measured at two times), one was $\alpha = .75$, six were between $\alpha = .73$ and .70, and the five remaining measures had alphas ranging between .48 and .69.

The dimensions most affected at time 1 were reassurance of worth (i.e., the recognition of one's competence, skills, and value by others), attachment (i.e., the emotional closeness from which one derives a sense of security), and social integration (i.e., a sense of belonging to a group that shares similar interests, concerns, and recreational activities). At time 2, the most affected dimensions were reliable alliance (i.e., the assurance that others can be counted upon for tangible assistance), opportunity for nurturance (i.e., the sense that others rely upon one for their well-being), attachment, and social integration. Caution is required.

Univariate Statistics

Because our objective was to describe our data in detail but in a simple way, we used the correlation which is a univariate approach to statistical analysis. However, univariate statistics cannot help in detecting more complex relationships involving for example more than two variables at a time. This means that it is possible that the relationship (or the absence of a relationship) between two variables can be explained by a unknown third variable. Consequently, caution should be exercised in interpreting our results.

---

[6]We considered reliability for the Project Involvement Index as adequate for a two-item measure.
